GARDEN PROJECTS
IN A WEEKEND™

GARDEN PROJECTS IN A WEEKEND™

Ali Ward

Sterling Publishing Co., Inc.
New York

Library of Congress Cataloging-in-Publication Data available

10 9 8 7 6 5 4 3 2 1

First published in Great Britain in 2002
by Hamlyn, a division of Octopus Publishing Group Ltd
2–4 Heron Quays, London E14 4JP

Copyright book design and illustrations
© Octopus Publishing Group Ltd 2002

Copyright © text Ali Ward 2002

Distributed in the United States and Canada by
Sterling Publishing Co., Inc.
387 Park Avenue South, New York, NY 10016

"In a Weekend" is the trademark property of Sterling
Publishing Co., Inc. and is used by permission

Printed and bound in China

All rights reserved. No part of this work may be reproduced
or utilized in any form or by any means, electronic or
mechanical, including photocopying, recording or by any
information storage and retrieval system, without the prior
written permission of the publisher.

Sterling ISBN 0-8069-9099-6

CONTENTS

INTRODUCTION

In the Utopian world that I long to inhabit, every one of my garden design clients would allow me an unlimited budget. They would own beautiful properties overlooking rolling acres of countryside and have a driving urge to re-landscape their entire garden in one gigantic, flamboyant gesture. Such are the dreams of garden designers. The reality, of course, is different. I have designed gardens no larger than an average sitting room, gardens on such steep slopes that they would make rather good ski runs, and been faced with unpromising, boggy plots.

Opposite This is a perfect, relaxed vista. The dark, lush planting entices the viewer up the path, towards the gate.

More often than not, a client will only want a small part of their garden redesigned, but considering small areas of garden without an overview of the whole is a recipe for disaster. Don't make this mistake! The 24 projects are, of course, the heart of the book, but it is the chapters that precede them that will make them a success. The chapters 'Design Essentials' and 'Assessing and Planning' will help you look at your garden with new eyes and assess objectively what you have – and what is missing. You might be planning a new plot from scratch or you might have a good overall scheme that needs that finishing touch to bring it to life. Either way, one of these projects will be an inspirational starting point on the road to a great garden.

The key to any of these projects is to think before you dig. It is tempting to dive straight in, but your enthusiasm will be short-lived if the feature you have painstakingly built ends up in the wrong place, facing the wrong way or at the wrong scale for your garden. No matter how good the design or the construction is, it will always look amateurish and out of place. Siting a feature is rather like 'Pin the Tail on the Donkey' – put it in the wrong place and, no matter how great-looking the

tail, the donkey is always going to look silly! Where helpful, the projects each include advice on siting, and I always find that trying out ideas on a scale plan (see page 32) saves a lot of second thoughts later.

These projects are designed to fill one, two or three weekends. I soon realized that gauging which project fitted into which category was not going to be easy; everyone has different skill levels and speeds of working. There is no such thing as the average person and certainly not the average gardener, so I hope you will forgive me if you charge through a three weekend project in a couple of days or if it takes you half the summer to complete a two weekend project. But all the projects are within the reach of anyone with some practical aptitude. Each comes complete with a shopping list of raw materials and plants, a list of the tools you will need and instructions to take you clearly through each stage step by step. Read through the entire project first, and don't skip over any of the stages. It can be tempting to miss out the undercoat when painting, for example, but you will find the top finish will only last one season before it starts to peel. Guessing a measurement instead of looking for the tape

measure will mean your finished feature never quite looks right or, worse, doesn't work at all. Attention to detail is everything. Aim to enjoy the process of construction as much as you will enjoy the finished article.

Although each project is entirely self-contained, many also complement one another, and so I have included some ideas for combining two or more projects. Probably many more will suggest themselves as you develop ideas for your own garden, for a garden should be individual, and reflect *your* taste and lifestyle. Good garden designers will create a garden that feels entirely the client's own; in fact, a designer's job is to synthesize the thoughts, needs and desires of the client. In a book, the consultation can only be a one-sided process, but that does not mean that the results have to be standardized, off-the-peg clones. For the new gardener, these projects can be followed to the letter and will be a pleasing, professional-looking addition to a garden, but I hope that you will find ways of adapting them to reflect your own personal style and preferences. I would be thrilled to know that you are straying from the designs and making them your own.

Every garden I produce has recurring features. These elements go to make up a great garden. You might not need to include every one, but each essential adds a new dimension to your design.

DESIGN ESSENTIALS

INTRODUCTION

Your head is probably brimming with materials, colours and concepts that you'd like to try in your new garden. To coordinate all your ideas in a way that gives you a professional finish, we need to consider the garden essentials: height, paths, terraces, seating, shelter, water, heat and light, and the needs of children.

Although I've called these essentials, not all will apply to you and you need not think that you must incorporate every one in order to create a good garden. Some will be essential to you and others will have just a fleeting role.

Height is the first essential because it is the most important – a garden design that is entirely flat will have little appeal. The way in which you create that height will have to suit your own garden, but you will find projects to inspire from a pergola (page 112) to a willow structure (page 68).

The hard landscape elements of your plot will probably be the most expensive aspect, so think hard before you commit yourself to a particular type of paving or fencing, and make sure that the materials you choose are in sympathy with their surroundings.

Seating, water, shelter and lighting are all luxuries for your garden, but they will lift it out of the ordinary and into the excellent!

Before you embark on a project, consider how it will relate to the garden you already have and the essential items that you want to include. You might be looking for a feature to brighten a drab corner in an otherwise attractive garden, in which case the obelisk (page 80) or the water feature (page 62) are what you are looking for. Alternatively, you may need to make over your entire plot, in which case the courtyard project (page 73) may be just

Left This perfect combination of height and seating is glimpsed through a deliberate gap in the planting. Secret corners are always a delight to discover.

right for you. If you have a clear idea of which garden style you'd like, you may be considering a themed garden. The bamboo fence (page 97) is perfect for a Japanese look, or the bench (page 60) will fit beautifully into an elegant modern setting.

Deciding on your own style is half the battle, so look at each project in relation to your garden and don't be afraid to make changes to the materials recommended to suit the look you want. If all the projects look tempting and you don't know where to start, read all the essentials carefully and make a list of those that you feel apply to you. When you know what your garden needs, you can then select the right project.

Above Successful use of mixed materials such as slabs, stones and planting make this terrace worth viewing from the small wooden bench.

Left Ferns and rocks become sculptural features when displayed against a stark 'gallery' wall.

ADDING HEIGHT

This is perhaps the most important essential. It may be stating the obvious to say that the addition of height gives your garden another dimension, but thinking in three planes can really make your garden come alive. This is especially true in a new plot where you may not have the benefit of mature trees or shrubs.

How high?

Every garden should exist on several levels. There needs to be interest at ground level, planting level and eye level, and what catches the eye at the upper levels could be garden buildings, screens or decorative objects just as much as planting. The obelisk on page 80 and the pergola on page 112 can both support plants, but will add a different perspective to your garden just as soon as they are erected. Indeed, the obelisk needs nothing more than a little thought as to its colour to fulfil its role in drawing your interest upwards.

Don't be afraid of height. The most common mistake is to make vertical features too low, especially if you only have a small garden. If you only have a restricted space, make features tall but

Right This combination of steps, followed by an avenue of arches, demonstrates a bold use of height. Don't be afraid to be grand in your scale.

Left A glass obelisk will change colour as you move around it, some sides reflecting foliage and some sunlight.

Below Great proportions is what makes this vista enticing. It is important to make sure that the object at the end is positioned absolutely in the centre.

narrow, so that they are neither over-bearing nor too solid. The decorative screen, with its criss-cross of ivy (see page 65), and the oriental screen (page 97) also add height without solidity and give you a glimpse of the garden beyond.

Using vertical accents

In a larger garden, vertical accents can be bold and architectural: yew hedges or pleached avenues, solid walls and impressive statuary, as well as loosely planted borders of large shrubs. If you are starting a new scheme, spend some of your budget on one or two mature plants to give height instantly.

Tall features can also be used to draw attention to an area. A path becomes more inviting if it is flanked by tree sentinels, or a new border will have instant appeal with the addition of three random-height obelisks. You can play with perspective, too. A series of decorative poles graded in height will make a path appear shorter if their height increases with distance, longer if their height decreases (and of course will have the opposite effect when viewed from the other end).

❖ **Project Links**

Decorative screen pages 65–67

Obelisk pages 80–83

Oriental screen pages 97–99

Pergola pages 112–114

Design Essentials

PATHS

Unless your garden is tiny, or is laid completely with hard landscape materials, you will need at least one path to allow you to take in the whole garden without getting your feet wet. This description does make a path seem rather a mundane, utilitarian feature, but that does not do it justice. A path whose design and route are well thought out will let you direct the way in which your garden is viewed. Use it not only as a means of getting from A to B, but also to draw attention to a vista or view, or as a temptation to discover what is beyond. There is absolutely no need to limit yourself to one path, of course, but each should have a purpose and should seem to fit naturally into the overall layout, otherwise it will either stick out like a sore thumb or simply never be used.

Right Informality made practical – a loose gravel path gives access through this wildflower meadow.

Below Combining different materials with similar colours allows you to 'paint' with your paths, drawing patterns in the ground.

Paving materials

Paths should echo the existing materials of the garden and house. The sleeper path on page 115, for instance, combines grass, wood and small flowers, which makes it ideal for linking a lawn with an area covered with bark chippings, or for leading you towards a wooded area. If you like the idea of a knot garden with its box hedges (see page 84), then the path to it could also be in gravel, the same surface as around the knot. As a further link, you could plant a small box hedge along either side of the path.

Planning paths

Any of the children's projects in this book will need a path for access.

❖ **Project Links**

Knot garden pages 84–86

Sleeper path pages 115–117

Left Smaller paving units are perfect for creating curves and circles, as they lend themselves easily to the shape.

Below This formal path is strictly ordered, which is reflected in the regimented borders on either side.

However, there is one important thing to remember about children (and dogs) in relation to paths; they will not use them unless they take the most direct route between door and destination. It is quite futile to put in a curved path as the children will always run in a straight line.

To a lesser extent, this also applies to adults, especially when you are planning a path up to the front door or along a regular, 'purposeful' route, such as to the compost heap or the garden shed. But a meandering path will appeal to garden lovers who like nothing better than exploring what is around the next corner or discovering a new plant in flower. Walk around your garden several times before deciding a path's route. The answer may be pre-ordained if you are planning a new vista to an existing feature, but otherwise take note of your natural route around the garden, as this will probably show the best course.

Design Essentials

A TERRACED AREA

It would be very strange if you put a great deal of effort into creating a beautiful garden but didn't include somewhere to sit out and enjoy what you have accomplished. While a garden can be admired from inside, it is only when you sit quietly among the plants that you really appreciate its beauty, and a terrace is the most practical way to do this.

Right Coloured furniture can add a splash of excitement to an otherwise predominantly green scheme.

Right Two sentinel trees obscure the terrace from immediate view, giving it a feeling of privacy.

Size

The size of a terrace will depend on what you are going to use it for. If you want an outside dining room with quite a large table and half a dozen chairs, then you should allow at least 4 x 4m (12 x 12ft); but, if you are only envisaging a café table and chairs for two, then 2m (6 or 7ft) in either direction should be enough.

Terracing materials

The material you use for your terrace will depend on what complements your house, the style of your garden and how the area is going to be used. If you are planning an outside eating area, for instance, you will need a solid,

flat surface so that your table won't wobble. Paving slabs are practical and blend in with most styles, but you might like to vary them with a contrasting material. The mosaic on page 100 is a more creative version of cobble or tile insets. Don't use too great a variety of materials or your terrace will look like a paving catalogue. Gravel is another good all-purpose surface (see the low-maintenance courtyard on page 73), but can be rather unstable for garden furniture unless it is well compacted. Bricks, paving blocks, bark and poured concrete are all other possibilities (see 'Hard Landscaping', page 130).

Siting a terrace

What is the best site for a terrace? Mostly, we envisage somewhere sunny and sheltered, and ideally with a little privacy. Close to the house is also convenient. But the garden may not offer all these attractions in one spot. The best suggestion I can make is – have two terraces! One, in the lee of the house or a convenient wall, might be ideal to catch the morning sun and tempt you to breakfast outdoors. The other could be at the other end of the garden, reached by an inviting path and surrounded by plants whose scent is heightened at dusk – an idyll on summer evenings. If an otherwise ideal site is inclined to be windy, use a planted screen such as a hedge or a pierced trellis; wind will go up and over a solid barrier and make matters worse.

Above In this garden one terrace leads into another which is a great way to absorb a slope into a design.

Below left Simplicity itself, a terrace can be as uncomplicated as just a bench and gravel.

❖ **Project Links**
Low-maintenance courtyard pages 73–75

Mosaic pages 100–102

SEATING

I can't think of one garden I have designed or visited that did not contain seating. Every room in your house has a resting place and so should your garden.

Seating types

Your choice of seat should enhance your garden. A slender, understated seat in tubular steel or sculptured wire would suit an elegant, minimal

scheme, but a walkway planted with traditional herbaceous borders might best lead to a large hardwood seat in a classical style. Whatever you choose, it should be comfortable and durable as well as look good. The oak bench on page 60 is a good example of a style that can be accommodated in a great variety of settings, and having made it yourself it will be above the usual run of seats found in every garden centre and furniture store.

When choosing a table and chairs for outside dining, the same considerations of style apply, but also be aware of the length of time you are likely to sit on the chairs. An ornate metal chair may look pretty and will be fine for a

quick coffee break, but for those long summer lunches you will need more commodious chairs with arms and preferably cushions!

Using seating in a colour scheme

Seating is an excellent way to introduce colour into a predominantly green scheme, but choose the colour you will use wisely. A pale colour will leap out, while a dark colour will recede into the background. Try to pick up on other features in the garden. For example, a border with predominantly blue planting will be enhanced by a bench in a similar shade. Choosing a contrasting colour will make a seat

Above A table and chairs in just the right shade of acid green to complement the lime planting.

Right Is it a seat or a sculpture? Beautiful craftsmanship makes this slate form a stunning resting place with *Buxus* balls marking its position.

❖ **Project Links**

Camomile seat pages 52–53

Oak bench pages 60–61

Herb steps pages 87–89

Turf sculpture pages 103–105

stand out against its surroundings. If you must have green, choose a pale acid-green or blue-green. Black is a great shade, and will fit in with almost any scheme.

Positioning seating

When deciding where to position a heavy chair or bench, try out the site first with an easily portable seat, or just crouch down to sitting height. Is there anything worth viewing? Why would you want to sit there? You need a reason to take the journey to the seat; make sure that you have one.

Non-standard seating

There are plenty of other types of seating that can be included in the garden. The camomile seat on page 52 is a marvellous piece of rural craft which provides the added pleasure of sitting on a scented cushion of green. This is a permanent fixture, but at the other end of the scale you can sling a hammock between two trees (or posts) for the ultimate in outdoor naps.

The structural design of your garden can also incorporate ad hoc seats. Retaining walls around ponds or borders or long, low steps make natural places to sit – the herb steps on page 87 and the turf sculpture on page 103 will both provide simple resting places. They also have the advantage of being there whenever you need them, brief resting places on bright winter days or an encouragement to loiter in the garden when you can't be bothered to get out of the deckchair.

Left A brick path leads to an elegant powder blue bench, framed by the wall behind it.

Below left The clashing vibrant colours of the plants would overwhelm a seat in any other colour. This is a brave choice, done with success

Design Essentials

SHELTER

Gardens are often promoted as 'outdoor rooms', but the problem with this is that seasonal changes and weather conditions limit the amount of time that it is possible to sit outside. The way to expand this time is to provide yourself with a garden shelter. This might be anything from a temporary canopy to a home-from-home summerhouse. Shelters of all sorts also provide a useful element of height in your garden (see pages 12–13).

Types of shelter

Right A summerhouse is an enticing reward at the culmination of a vista.

Starting with the most elaborate and expensive, a summerhouse is really like another room to your house, located away from the hustle and bustle of household life. While I always imagine myself lounging in a peaceful retreat made specifically for reading, it can just as easily be an office or workspace. A summerhouse is not just to be enjoyed from the inside but also provides interest in the garden as a whole. A well-designed and well-constructed summerhouse can be the central feature to a design, sited at the end of a magnificent vista, or hidden in woodland, accessible only by a narrow pathway, to give ultimate privacy.

Below Climbing plants help to blend this shelter in with the surrounding garden.

Not all of us have the budget for a summerhouse, but a gazebo or pergola can have similar uses and be just as appealing. A pergola is usually a timber structure constructed to give support to climbing plants which then

form a semi-solid roof overhead, whereas a gazebo is an open-sided pavilion with a solid roof. Both will give shelter for the resting gardener from either baking sunlight or pouring rain. Even in the cold winter months it is pleasurable to sit in a gazebo and, although partially open to the elements, the roof will provide enough shelter to make the rest a pleasant one. The unusually shaped pergola on page 112 doubles as a shield to a sheltered sitting or dining area.

Finally, your shelter can be as simple as a canvas canopy erected during the summer months (see page 90). This will afford you all the shelter of its more expensive cousins, but you can be much more flamboyant in your choice of colour and style, providing a feature that is visually stunning but also useful.

Above More of an excuse for growing roses than a shelter, but there can be no better shady spot on a warm afternoon.

Left Comfortable cushions in this summerhouse make a great spot for a relaxing afternoon. The path echoes the shape of the summerhouse, settling it into its surroundings.

❖ **Project Links**

Sun canopy pages 90–93

Pergola pages 112–114

WATER

Is a water feature a garden essential? To be honest, I don't think it is – a garden will be no less inspiring if it is made with or without one. However, water has a magnetic appeal and, just as trees and garden structures add height, it does introduce a whole new dimension to the garden. It does not even have to be running water, as still water contributes a constant, subtle movement. A breeze will cause gentle ripples, and sunlight reflecting off a flat surface will give off shards of sparkling light that will ricochet around your garden.

Types of water feature

Right This spouting lion's head might look a little stark if it weren't for the lush foliage planting softening the edges of the water feature.

Try to be imaginative with water. Any vessel can be incorporated into your feature, as long as it is watertight. Consider anything from fish tanks to watering cans, fed by copper pipes, glass rods or steel tubes. The two projects included in this book are very different, the first a small, simply planted pool that would fit into any garden (see page 62) and the other a stylized, original interpretation of a spring and stream (see page 122).

Siting water features

Water features of any kind generally like a bit of sunshine. It helps to keep the water fresh. Heavy shade from trees can be suffocating as well as creating problems when the leaves drop. Bear this in mind when deciding where to position any water feature. Before you start the hard work of excavating for a pool, also consider whether it will interrupt any natural routes around the garden; if it does, it will be annoying rather than appealing.

Safety around water

Children and water together are a difficult problem. Water features are appealing, especially to the very young, but they are also incredibly dangerous. If you have any doubts about a feature, leave it out – you can always add it at a later date when your children have grown up a bit. There are some water features, however, that *are* safe for children and that

work particularly well in small spaces. Water running over a solid object such as a sphere or pot will give you all the movement you need as well as water's other great advantage, sound. This is especially useful in town gardens where there may be permanent background noise. The sound of running water will go some way to covering the hum, or at least distracting attention from it.

If you install a feature that requires a pump, then you will need an electricity supply. This is not a job for the amateur gardener; always use a professional electrician and make provision for this cost in your budget.

Above Each of the three level drops in this feature will produce a slightly different note, creating a soothing background noise.

Left Reflection is one of the greatest appeals of water in a garden, and can be achieved with the simplest of pond and architectural grasses.

❖ **Project Links**

Water feature pages 62–64

Pebble stream pages 122–125

HEAT AND LIGHT

There is no reason why a garden should not be enjoyed during the evening and night just as it is during the daytime. It is quite marvellous to be outside on a crisp spring evening if you have a fire to snuggle around.

Right Small spot uplighters between each topiary pot give this garden added impact.

Don't relegate bonfires to rubbish-burning areas near the compost heap. A fire pit in the centre of a terrace will be a magnet, and even in the height of summer the heat soon goes from the sun and the allure of a crackling flame is undeniable. If real fires are too much work, there are plenty of gas-powered heaters now on the market. Once the preserve of restaurants and bars, you will be amazed at the difference they make. You will be able to stay in your shirtsleeves all night, especially if there is an enclosing boundary, even a hedge, to help retain the heat.

Extending the daylight hours

Lighting makes your garden accessible after dark. It can also set the mood. Bright spotlights are practical to illuminate a car park, but if you point them up into the canopy of a tree the illuminated network of branches becomes a sculptural feature. There are plenty of types of lighting to choose from and it is simply a matter of finding one to work with your garden.

Try to use a variety of lighting in your garden. Several lights along a pathway are excellent, especially if you mix them with spotlights picking out a tree or an attractive feature. My favourite light, though, is candlelight. Candles give a garden a magical feeling. They are also very inexpensive and can be as simple as a line of tea lights along the edge of a terrace or hung in jars in a tree.

> ❖ **Project Link**
> Lighting pages 76–77

CHILDREN IN THE GARDEN

Children bring a whole host of considerations to garden planning and, if you are lucky enough to have children, they have probably claimed the garden for their own already. The only way you will reclaim any of it for yourselves is to create an area that is devoted to their pleasure.

For very small children, keep construction materials as even and smooth as possible – learning to walk on cobbles is quite a task – and don't even consider any open water. This does not mean you can't have any sort of water in the garden, but even hidden reservoirs must be securely locked. Make sure that the access to any play area is safe and don't expect children to follow winding paths; straight wide access is what is called for. Play areas should, of course, be kept as safe as possible. Don't use fencing with pointed tops or plant stakes near play areas. A thick layer of bark mulch on the ground will cushion falls; it is safe and looks neat.

Making the garden child-friendly

Lawn is always a good bet with children and, if you have the room, a turf sculpture (see page 103) will provide hours of fun as the hills become dens and alien landscapes. I have also included a couple of projects specifically for children that will enhance the garden, rather than need to be hidden away. The living wigwam (see page 68), a perennial favourite, is fun to make, and you only have to look at the fort (see page 94) to know how popular it would be. While there is a lot of work in the construction, it will be the most popular place, summer or winter, from as soon as they can climb until they leave home!

Left This would have been my ideal wendyhouse as a child. The symmetry and soft colour make it elegant enough for any garden.

Below left Play equipment needn't be bright and vulgar. This wooden climbing frame sits subtly within a border scheme.

❖ **Project Links**

Living wigwam pages 68–69

Play fort pages 94–96

Turf sculpture pages 103–105

Assessing a plot is essential as a starting point, whether you are adding another feature or designing an entire garden from scratch. It may sound intimidating, but it just consists of learning to stand still, put your ideas on hold for a while and look at what you have to work with.

ASSESSING AND PLANNING

DRAWING A PLAN

The easiest way to take long measurements is with a surveyor's tape. If you don't have one, you can make your own by measuring off a long length of rope with an ordinary dressmaking tape or long ruler, marking every 50cm or 18in with a circle of sticky tape. Alternatively, if you think you can pace evenly, take one stride as 1m or 1yd. You may have to practise to get it even enough to measure the garden this way.

Measure each boundary and the diagonals between, and then draw up the garden's outline on graph paper. The size of your garden will determine the size of squares you choose, but one square should correspond to 1m or 1yd.

Include any part of your house that forms part of the boundary. The position of doors and windows is relevant from the point of view of access to the garden and framed picture views, and important all year. In garden design terms a 'directed' view, such as one from a window or down an avenue, is known as a vista. You may find it helps to draw faint lines that run out into the garden from either side of your windows to indicate the vista. When you come to play around with the position of a project, you can then see if the feature is directly in line with a vista. It then becomes the 'reward' at the end of your vista.

Working to the same scale, measure (don't guess) and mark in the areas of hard landscaping, such as paths and terraces. Add a note of the type of material they are constructed from.

Add in other existing features such as garden structures, pools and flower borders. You may like to take an inventory of the borders' contents. If there are particularly large plants, label them on the plan; otherwise make a list down the side (a simple description such as 'spiky blue flowers', 'tall pink bells' or 'evergreen shrub' is just as useful if you don't know the plants' names).

The way to work out the position of features that are not close to the boundaries is by triangulation. This may sound like back-to-school geometry, but is quite simple.

To position a tree, for example, take a measurement from the trunk to a known point on your plan, such as a corner of the garden or edge of a building. Take a second measurement from another static position to the

Right If possible, view your garden from an upstairs window. This helps to get an idea of the proportions of the plot and what is worth keeping.

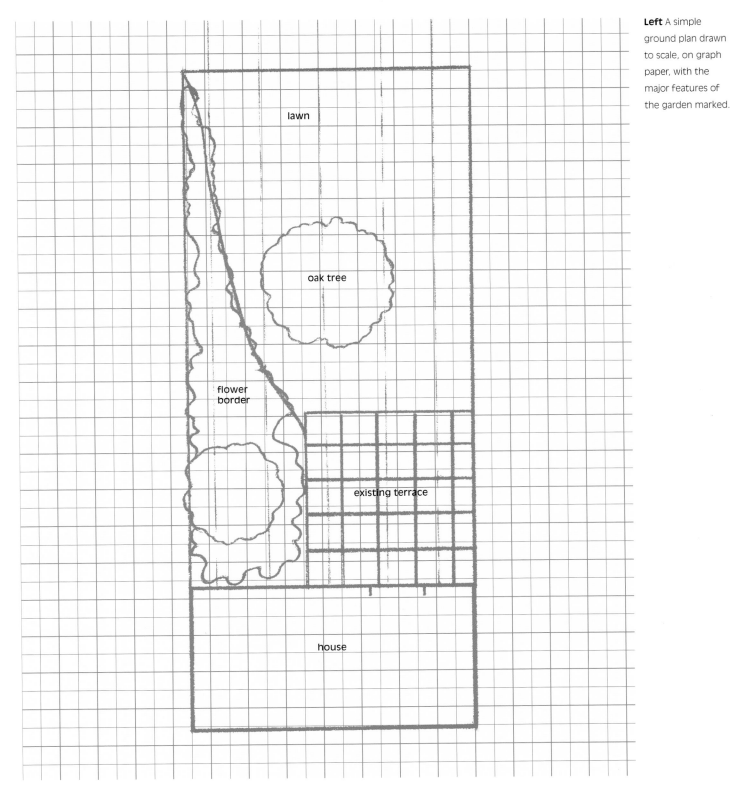

lawn

oak tree

flower
border

existing terrace

house

Left A simple
ground plan drawn
to scale, on graph
paper, with the
major features of
the garden marked.

trunk. Then, on your plan, using a
compass with the point on each of the
static places in turn, scribe two arcs
that correspond to the measurements
you have taken. Where the arcs cross is
the trunk's position. The canopy of the
tree is also an important consideration
as it will provide shelter as well as cast-
ing shadows. Take a measurement of
the diameter of the canopy and add it
to the plan. A simple circle drawn with
a compass is enough, but if you like
you can then make the edges of the
canopy rough, for a more realistic
representation.

A GARDEN RECORD

As well as recording the physical features in your garden, you can use your plan to indicate other influences in your garden.

Sun, shade, wind and rain

Opposite This garden runs from deep shade to sunlight.
Below A garden corner shaded by mature trees is perfect for lush, shade-loving plants.

Some gardens have lots of weather! Coastal sites have their share of wind problems, gardens in certain areas will suffer from high levels of rainfall, and some, at the other end of the spectrum, won't get enough and will be prone to drought.

Consider the movement of the sun throughout the day. How do the light levels within the garden change? Make a note of areas of heavy shade and which areas are sunny at which times of the day.

Over the course of a few days, note the direction of prevailing winds. Wind problems can be exacerbated by buildings. You may find that the prevailing wind forced down a corridor between two buildings will produce a wind-tunnel effect, making a draughty area within your garden. Note any problems on your plan.

Borrowed landscape

No garden exists totally in isolation. Any feature that is not actually inside the boundary of your garden but should be taken into account in the design is known as borrowed

landscape. Look beyond the garden at the surroundings: are you overlooked by a building or overshadowed by a monstrous electricity pylon? Or is there perhaps a feature that is pleasing to the eye: a neighbour's tree or view over the surrounding countryside? Make a note of these on your plan so you can include or hide these features within the final design.

Contours

Not every garden is flat. Yours may already be terraced on several levels, or you may be contemplating what to do with a bare slope. It is necessary to calculate drops in level, and if you are redesigning a whole garden it would be worth drawing up a cross-section of your plot, to show it in profile. For the

projects in this book, however, it will be enough to note the changes in level and to check on the flatness of small areas when you come to consider the site for an individual project.

Photographs

Photographs are very useful in assessing a garden's possibilities – the lens throws up angles and views in a way that is quite different from just looking at a familiar scene. Start with views looking down the length of the garden. You are not looking for pretty scenes: these photographs will be a practical aid, so you need to catalogue the unattractive corners as well as the beautiful parts. Move up the garden and take some more photographs looking back in the other direction.

Trees

Trees are a gift to the garden and should be treasured, but the roots must not be disturbed; if you do, it may cause harm to the tree. It is possible to put posts in the ground fairly close to a tree but be prepared to dig very carefully. You may need to adjust a post's position to avoid cutting into a root, so work out the effect this may have on the whole project before you start.

With large trees, the other advantage and disadvantage is the shade they create. You will find that the deep shade underneath their canopy is not suitable for all plants to thrive in. It is not like the transient shade in other areas of your plot that may only occur for a few hours a day. A large tree will often have some shade at its base all day. This may be a disadvantage, but a shady spot to site a seat in can also be a godsend, especially in a particularly sunny site.

USING YOUR PLAN

You may have a particular project in mind, or you may be looking for inspiration. Either way, your plan can help you see how a feature would sit within the rest of the garden. You can pencil in different routes for paths and steps, or sketch in pergolas or pools in various sizes and shapes.

An extra help is to make a template of any proposed feature. Draw a plan of it on a separate sheet of graph paper (to the same scale, or chaos may ensue!), cut it out and move it round the garden plan to see the effect in different locations. In the example opposite the knot garden project (see page 84) has been used.

If you find that the site you would like to use for a feature means that you have to cover over an area of existing border or terrace, don't immediately dismiss the site. It is purely a matter of priority. Does the siting of your feature warrant the sacrifice of what exists there already? Always be open to negotiation with yourself.

Proportion and impact

With your planned feature in a promising position, consider how it relates to its surroundings. Is it overshadowed by an existing structure or building? Does its proximity to them make it look small and insignificant? Alternatively, is it so large that it dwarfs everything around it? The garden and its features must be balanced, each one in pleasing scale to the things around it.

Your photographs can help here. Lay a sheet of drafting film (or tracing paper or greaseproof paper) over the photograph and draw on the new feature or plants. Use known proportions in the photographs such as windows and fences as a guide to help you judge the heights of pergolas, plants, and so on, and remember that things will appear larger as they get nearer to the front of your picture. Don't try to draw plants too realistically; outline shapes will be adequate.

It is tempting to rush through this process – the garden awaits and your head is full of enthusiasm for the project you have chosen, but trying out your ideas on paper may save you a lot of heartache later on.

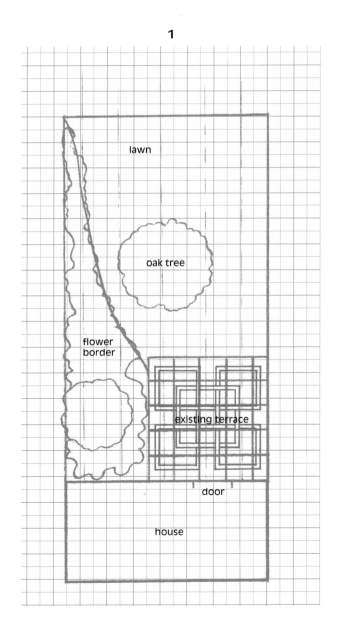

1

lawn

oak tree

flower border

existing terrace

door

house

CHOOSING THE BEST POSITION

1 The knot garden is where the terrace is currently located. It can be enjoyed from the house as the door lines up exactly with the central line of the knot garden, and there is enough space around it to allow access to the rest of the garden. The disadvantage is that the terrace will need to be moved.

2 The knot garden is left of the terrace. It can be admired from the windows and only a small section of the terrace will be sacrificed. However, some of the border will need to go and the garden may feel cramped at one end.

3 The knot garden is between the terrace and the tree. Only a small section of the terrace needs to be removed and the garden aligns

pleasingly when viewed from the door. The border can stay and would look even better extended slightly. The drawback is the shadow created by the tree, which may need thinning.

Option 3 is best. It doesn't involve moving the terrace, it maintains the vista and it divides the garden attractively into three areas – terrace, knot garden and lawn – creating a journey through the garden.

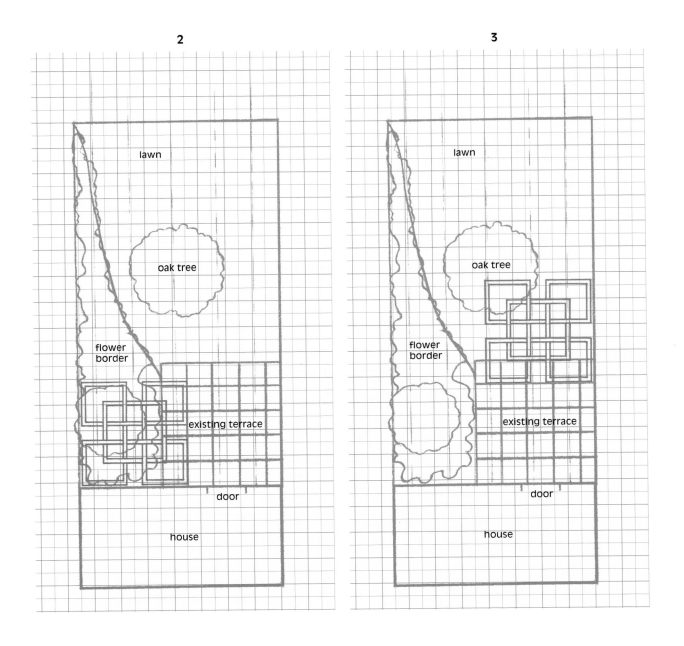

In the world of landscape gardening 'hard landscaping' refers to anything that isn't alive, and is most commonly used to describe the laying of groundcover surfaces.

HARD LANDSCAPING

USING HARD LANDSCAPE MATERIALS

A garden that is constructed entirely of plants – such as a wildflower meadow or flower borders with lawns – may seem great in theory, but soon you may find that you would like stepping stones so you can get through your borders without getting your feet wet or squashing plants, or you might like a seat, and a path to it, to enjoy your garden in comfort. Then you may discover the delights of a fragrant rose arbour or a dry-stone wall to increase the types of habitats for your plants. Hard landscape combines the practical needs you have for your garden with the artistic element you want to introduce.

Choosing the right hard landscape materials

Right This garden mixes several shades of terracotta in brick and tile, giving a coordinated look.

Below Materials that are different in colour and texture can create stunning combinations, such as this pale wooden path snaking through a blue paddle-stone bed.

Hard landscape is also the part of your design that will probably cost you the most. The first decision you will need to make is what type of hard landscape you want for your garden. If you have a practical mind, this may seem the wrong way round; surely you should first look at what you can afford! I disagree. Always start by getting the design right. The choice of hard landscape materials is the backbone of your design. Get it wrong and you will be stuck with your mistake. If you make the wrong choice of plant, if it ends up in the wrong place or the colour doesn't match, it is easy to deal with and can even be thrown away and put down to experience. Make a mistake with a whole terrace or fence and you're stuck with it!

Many of the projects in this book include an element of hard landscaping. Although a specific material is given, like a recipe, you can often substitute another that would better fit your requirements or taste. For example, you could choose to concrete rather than terracotta for paths.

Choosing the right materials for your garden needs some careful thought. Go out and take notes on the

type of material that your house is constructed of; look at the colour of your window frames and any other structures such as conservatories, sheds or fences. A material that complements its surroundings will be much more successful than one that looks totally alien. Some materials set a certain style, which you may want to pick up on for a themed garden; others work best in a modern setting, or in a rural garden. In a small area, it is best to limit the variety of hard landscape

materials you introduce, as more than one or two can look confusing and cluttered.

On a practical note, consider the shape of the area you are intending to work with. If you are planning a sinuous path or a curving terrace, you will find small units of paving much less trouble to lay than large ones which will have to be cut to fit. If you want to cover a children's play area, bark would be a softer surface to break falls than paving or gravel.

Above left Decking allows us to raise walkways with ease. This path appears to float among the foliage.

Above right Reclaimed materials such as this stone can be given a new lease of life. Set on end, it creates perfect planting pockets for sempervivums.

Gravel

Style of garden Almost any, from contemporary to traditional. A must for Japanese gardens.

Available in Several grades and every colour you can imagine, from traditional honey colour through white marble to crushed glass and even brightly coloured chips.

Combines best with Just about anything. Traditional gravel is particularly good next to terracotta brick and small, pale gravel is essential for a Japanese theme.

Use for Terraces or paths. It also has the bonus of being inexpensive and easy to lay (see page 133).

Shapes Any. The ultimate utility material.

Stone

Style of garden Classical and formal, traditional look with straight lines.

Available in Slabs. You can get very good fake stone slabs, although the price difference is surprisingly little.

Combines best with Painted walls and traditional properties.

Use for Terraces, paths, steps. (To lay paving, see page 134.)

Shapes Squares, oblongs, any shape that uses strong, straight lines. Good laid in a random pattern.

Granite setts or slate

Style of garden Traditional material, but can be used in a contemporary way, so it will fit either scheme.

Available in Slate as tiles and granite as setts or cobbles.

Combines best with Painted walls or traditional buff stone. The grey-blue colour also works well alongside steel and reflective materials.

Use for Paths and terraces (see page 134).

Shapes Small cobbles good for curves and circles; larger slate pieces better for straight lines.

Terracotta

Style of garden Traditional cottage garden with mellow colours, or a Mediterranean theme that mixes terracotta with vivid blues and oranges.

Available in Bricks, paving slabs, chips that look like gravel.

Combines best with Honey-coloured gravel of any grade.

Use for Paths, edging for lawns, terraces and borders, or walls. (See page 136 for laying terracotta tiles and page 138 for laying brick paving.)

Shapes Good for both circles and straight edges. Can be laid in lots of patterns including herringbone and basket weave.

Concrete

Style of garden Contemporary and minimalist, a modern theme makes best use of concrete.

Available in Paving slabs, usually square; liquid mix for pouring into a mould (see page 137).

Combines best with Modern properties.

Use for Dwarf walls, terraces, paths or utility areas.

Shapes A wet mix will make any shape. Paving slabs are not easy to use for curved shapes. The cut edge of a slab is a different texture from the cast edge (a feature of the seat in the minimalist garden on page 118).

Timber

Style of garden A natural woodland or contemporary look.

Available in Timber lengths or pre-made square units either planed (smooth) or unplaned (rough). Can be painted or stained almost any colour.

Combines best with Bark chippings or glass chippings.

Use for Decking, raised walkways, bridges, pergolas and fences.

Shapes Very versatile, can be adapted to most shapes.

Bark

Style of garden Informal, woodland or meadow.

Available in Chippings.

Combines best with Timber deck or lawn.

Use for Paths, play spaces or seating areas (see page 139).

Shapes Can be contained by a timber edge to make an orderly shape or left loose for a natural look.

BUYING HARD LANDSCAPE MATERIALS

Once you have settled on your material you will need to find it. The easiest place to start is your local DIY or garden centre. They will probably have reasonably priced materials but the range may be a little limited. They tend to stock what is most fashionable at the moment and you may have to look a little harder if you want originality. A local builders' merchant will hold a reasonable stock of assorted materials and may also be able to order more interesting products for you.

You may want to go direct to a supplier. Look through the advertisements in gardening magazines and search the Web. You may stumble across things you never knew about, and ordering straight from the manufacturer can prove less expensive. For items such as gravel and stone, you can go directly to a quarry, or for bark chippings to a saw mill, although you may have to order in large quantities.

Finally, one of my favourite places to shop is reclamation yards. These are becoming more common and the advantage is that you can find something a little out of the ordinary. They are indispensable if you are creating a garden with a traditional look. You may also discover a bargain, but don't assume because the material is second-hand that it will be inexpensive.

Knowing how much of a particular material to order can give gardeners a headache, but if you take the dimensions of the area you are working on to your supplier they will usually be only too happy to work it out for you.

Right These terracotta bricks are very old. If you are trying to recreate the same look don't be tempted to use wall bricks as they will disintegrate in frost. Buy a specialist material.

Top Timber is a marvellous garden material. It is inexpensive and makes stunning features such as this oriental-style bridge.

Above You can pick up cheap material from reclamation yards. Use them imaginatively to create combinations such as this.

Some things to remember

- All softwood for outdoor features should be tanalized – pressure-treated by being impregnated with preservative under a vacuum. Tanalized timber is guaranteed for 15–30 years and should be used even if you intend to colour with another preservative. Tanalized timber is readily available from timber yards. You may find stock at your local DIY centre but it is much more expensive to purchase this way.

- When you are buying your timber make sure that square-section lengths are straight. Timber has a tendency to twist, which will make it very difficult to screw to flat boards.

- Nails for all outdoor projects should be galvanized and screws should be zinc-plated. These will not rust.

- With all hard landscape groundcover such as terraces, patios and paths, make sure that they slope imperceptibly away from the house or boundary walls to an area of free drainage. A slope of 1:70 is ideal, or a drop of 1cm for every metre (½in per yard).

- Be aware of the damp-proof course (DPC) on your property. Never allow any hard landscaping to go higher than 15cm (6in), or one brick course, below your damp-proof course.

- When levelling a slab use a rubber mallet, not a hammer, to hit the slab, or you may find that the slab cracks.

- Invest in a large spirit level. Your terrace or path will not look professional if every slab tilts in a different direction.

- Lastly, always employ a professional electrician to install electricity outdoors. Wiring in the garden should never be attempted by even a competent amateur.

Designing gardens is exciting and selecting materials is thrilling, but nothing compares to selecting the plants for your garden. This is the element that will bring the plot to life and allow you to express your personal taste and creativity.

PLANTS AND PLANTING

Plants and Planting

PLANTS

The choice of plants available is quite bewildering. I find selecting the plants for a project the most exciting part and could easily get carried away. Just when I believe I have decided on my favourites, there will be a new introduction and I am put in a quandary again. The plants recommended for these projects are all good growers and hard workers. Unless you are a confident and experienced grower, it is better to stick to plants that are readily available and easily grown. Their success is more likely to be assured and will encourage you to expand your knowledge and try some more unusual varieties.

Healthy plants

You don't need to be a plant expert but it's certainly worth learning a little about the conditions a plant needs before you buy it. Fortunately for the amateur gardener, if you purchase plants from a nursery or garden centre, most of the information that you need will be marked on a label on the pot. While most plants are content in average conditions, if the site for your chosen project is special in some way, it's worth finding plants that will suit those conditions. You may, for example, have a heavily shaded plot. Placing Scabiosa in an area of deep shade won't kill it, but it definitely won't thrive, whereas Hemerocallis will happily tolerate shade for half the day.

From top left
Zantedeschia aethiopica, Scabiosa 'Crimson Cushion', *Scabiosa caucasica* 'Clive Greaves', *Hemerocallis* 'Yellow Frosting'.

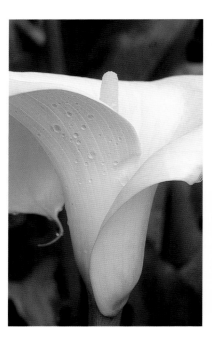

Soil

Apart from sun or shade, the most common cause of unhappy plants is the wrong soil condition. A few plants, such as rhododendrons, need acid soil and there are some plants, such as Cosmos and Dianthus, that will tolerate alkaline soil. Texture is important too: you need to feel the earth. The ideal soil should be friable, a rich brown colour, and full of organic matter. You can improve the soil you have by digging in organic matter, like rotted manure, but if there is a fundamental problem like waterlogging or if the soil is very free-draining, save yourself the heartache of fighting nature and search out plants that are adapted to the conditions you have.

CHOOSING THE RIGHT PLANT

There are a few things to remember when you are shopping for plants. Garden centres will always hold a large supply of plants that are in bloom. They will be positioned at the entrance and exit in wonderful displays to grab your attention and it takes an iron will not to be swayed. When plant-hunting for a particular project, make the visit to the garden centre or nursery project-specific if you can, and write a list to remind yourself what you are shopping for.

Once you have passed the seasonal pretties and found a display of the plant on your list, you then have another dilemma. Which out of the plants available do you choose? It is tempting to reach for the largest specimen; it feels like good value for money, but in plants bigger is not always better. It is possible that the plant has been packed tightly between other plants when growing and become etiolated – reaching for the little available light, not vigorous growth, has made it tall and thin. If you study it you will probably find it has very little foliage at its base and the stem may be weak and distorted. Look instead for a plant that is a good average height compared to its neighbours. Check its shape. Is it even all the way round? Does it have a pleasing symmetry? Always go for a plant that is smaller rather than larger, as shape is more important than size.

Once you are happy with the aesthetics of your plant, cast an eye over the pot and compost. If the compost is dry and coming away from the sides of the pot, its only hope of salvation is a plunge in a bucket of water; it is so dried out that water from the top would just run right through. Make sure that the soil is not too wet; if you press your hand into the compost

there shouldn't be puddles of water and the compost should have a pleasant earthy smell like a winter's morning.

Check the surface of the compost. Don't buy if it is a matted mess of weeds. If the compost is very loose and fresh, gently tug the plant from its pot to make sure that it hasn't recently been potted on. The plant should be established but not crowded.

Finally, give the plant a good check over. Look carefully for any unwanted bugs or strange-looking patches on the foliage. If in doubt, ask. Any good supplier will be happy to help you make sure that what you are buying is a good-quality plant.

Above Colour themed borders need plenty of skill to execute well, especially if you are using white. Don't underestimate the importance of foliage as a foil for the blooms.

Left A low hedge of chives makes a striking statement next to its larger cousin, the ornamental *Allium*.

Plants and Planting

PLANTING OUT

The plants you bring home will, hopefully, have been tended by professionals, their every need taken care of. Once a plant has been purchased, however, it is all too often underfed and left to fend for itself. If you want maximum growth and flower from your plants, then give them the attention they need. Almost all plants need exactly the same planting treatment, so the details are not repeated in every project, but you should always follow this procedure.

Above A subtle choice of plants that spans the breadth of yellow from acid *Nicotiana* to vibrant *Hemerocallis*, with a dash of purple lavender to keep the scheme from looking dull.

Right *Clematis* 'Nelly Moser' is the perfect companion for this tree. The tree's shade stops the colour of the flowers fading.

First, dig a planting hole that is twice the size of the pot the plant has been grown in. Refill the bottom of the hole with organic matter, such as well-rotted manure or multi-purpose compost mixed with the soil.

Take the plant out of its pot and place it in the hole so that the surface of the soil around the plant is level with the top of the hole. There are a few exceptions to this. Clematis are better buried more deeply, so that two or three of the buds on the stem are under the soil. This will give the plant a second chance if it suffers from clematis wilt. Wilt does not seem able to travel below ground, so should the plant die right back it will, with luck,

shoot again from below ground level. The other common exception is any rose or tree where the top growth of the plant has been grafted onto a different rootstock. There will be an obvious graft point, like a large callous, a little way up the stem. This needs to stay clear of the surface of the soil to avoid the upper plant putting down its own roots, bypassing the rootstock and reverting. Pot-grown plants can be planted at any time of the year, but trees or hedges are bought and planted as bare-root plants from mid-autumn to late winter.

Now refill the area around the plant with the soil that you originally dug out. If your soil is very poor in quality or textures mix some more compost into it. Firm the plant in well. If it is a large shrub or tree, do this with the heel of your boot. It might seem brutal, but as the plant is large it will be prone to rocking in the wind and can easily work itself loose.

Finally, water the plant, even if there has been rain recently. And don't just sprinkle a little water on the top of the plant; let the hose run into the roots. Your plant has just moved house; it will be thirsty.

Plant Care

Please don't walk away now feeling you have done everything. You will still need to keep an eye on plants for the first growing season to make sure that they are getting enough moisture as they establish their roots in the earth. Help them to perform for you by adding a little extra nourishment to

their diet. The choice of food is up to you: there are soluble feeds to add to your watering can, granular ones to mix into the soil, or just old-fashioned rotted manure spread around the base. Your plants will only need this extra food during the height of the growing season, from mid-spring to late summer.

If you choose every plant you buy wisely and plant it in the way I have recommended, I still can't promise you that it will grow – plants, like people, can be temperamental – but you will at least have done your best for it. From then on it's up to Mother Nature.

PLANTING IN CONTAINERS

Container gardening is often thought of as easier than working with traditional borders, but I don't think it is. Containers need constant monitoring to assess their moisture and nutrient levels. They can dry out very quickly, or easily become swamped by their occupants. Having said that, they are marvellously versatile and also allow you to grow plants that you may not otherwise be able to, such as tender plants or ones that need a soil different from your own garden soil.

The material a pot is made from may help or hinder plant growth. Terracotta looks great but it can easily dry out, so lining it with a plastic sheet will help prevent evaporation (remember to leave a drainage hole at the bottom). Plastic pots are good for holding moisture but don't have the good looks of terracotta or clay. Use them inside decorative planters, or hide them behind other, more attractive, containers or disguise with planting. Glazed pots are good all-rounders, but you have to make sure that the glaze colour or pattern complements, not clashes with, the planting and garden design. Metal planters can be very stylish, but they will absorb the heat which can cook the roots of the plant inside, so you will have to line the container with sacking or polystyrene tiles.

Wood is a great material. A wooden planter should be constructed of pressure-treated timber, when it should

Left This display of white Cosmos shows how stylish a single type and colour of plant can be.

Below Just because a pot is tall, don't feel the plant has to follow suit. A pendulous plant can look just as good.

last a good 15 years, but a lining of plastic between the compost and the wood will help ensure a long life.

Be creative

The bottom line when it comes to containers is that if it will hold compost then you can plant it! Anything from galvanized buckets to watering cans can be used – but remember if you are using an unusual container it will still need to have drainage holes in the bottom. When it comes to positioning your containers, try odd numbers in random sizes for an informal look, or repeat the same container several times for a formal feel. But perhaps my favourite use for containers is on either side of a path where one area of the garden gives way to the next. When choosing a container, size matters: the bigger the better; small pots suffer more from the problems highlighted than larger ones, so choose a pot larger than the one you think you need. Don't be timid about experimenting with containers: if it can hold compost you can plant in it, and if it grows it is suitable for planting in a container. Given the right pot, anything from snowdrops to an oak tree can be grown in a container, so use your imagination.

Above Anything goes! A wide section of bamboo looks stunning with a small spiky grass growing in it.

Right These agaves look fabulous when repeated in a formal line. The foliage will also throw intriguing shadows on the wall behind.

LAYING A LAWN

A lawn is so often taken for granted that it is easy to forget that grass is a plant and has much the same requirements as other plants: a good start in life for its roots, water, and the occasional feed to boost it.

Grass is graded from 'fine' to 'meadow'. Fine looks like a bowling green; it has a very rich green tone and each blade is narrow and sharp. But it is also not as tough, so unless you are a lawn connoisseur stick to the meadow variety – it will take a good deal of abuse and still look great.

You can order different types of turf from your local supplier. Make sure that the turf you buy is freshly cut. Don't buy from a garden centre that has a pallet of sods waiting to be sold; they will be either dried out or over watered and slimy. Ring a local turf supplier (look in the telephone directory) who will cut your turf and deliver it straightaway.

Sowing grass seed is less expensive than turf, but you will have to wait a little longer for the result. Sowing is best done in spring or early autumn, when shoots should germinate within a week or two.

What to do

Whichever method you choose, the preparatory steps are the same.

First, level the area to be grassed and rake out and remove any large stones. Then, 'penguin walk' over the area. This involves taking small flat-footed steps to ensure that the area is flat and without air pockets. Give it a light rake after this.

If you are sowing seed, you just need to scatter the seed according to the supplier's instructions. Keep the area watered and protect from birds and cats – I use strips of aluminium tied to canes so they rattle in the slightest breeze.

To turf, lay the first roll of turf out. It is easiest to start along a straight edge of a path or building if you have

one. Unroll the next turf beside it but so that it begins halfway down the side of the first. Continue in this way, creating a brick-wall or running-bond effect that will stagger the joins and avoid a series of continuous lines where the sods abut each other. Make sure that all the edges butt up tightly, and place

a long plank or scaffold board over each join and apply firm pressure to help it settle. Standing on a board will also avoid your feet denting the new-laid lawn.

Always water new turf for the first few weeks, until the sods are knitted to the ground and each other.

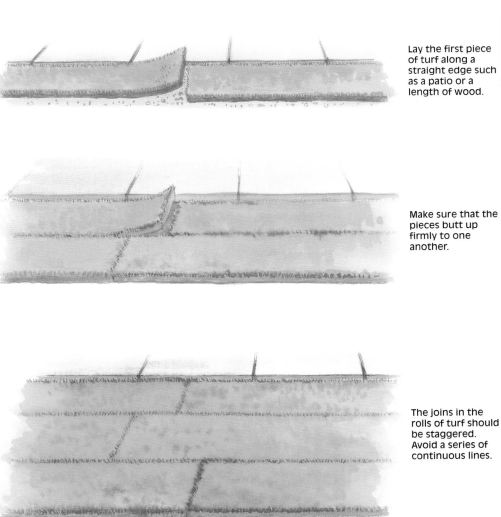

Lay the first piece of turf along a straight edge such as a patio or a length of wood.

Make sure that the pieces butt up firmly to one another.

The joins in the rolls of turf should be staggered. Avoid a series of continuous lines.

There is no denying the satisfaction of completing a project. These one-weekend designs should tempt you into improving your garden – and when you are full of confidence from this chapter there are loads more to test your enthusiasm.

ONE WEEKEND PROJECTS

CAMOMILE SEAT

Camomile seats can be found in some of the oldest garden designs. Since this 'living seat' cannot be moved, it will always provide somewhere to pause and rest for a moment, even on winter days when all the other garden furniture has been put away. It also gives you an opportunity to direct the attention of whoever is sitting in it to a particular vista or feature.

Apart from its medicinal use, camomile has a pleasing scent and the cultivar *Chamaemelum nobile* 'Treneague' grows so low and flat that it is perfect for using as a lawn or seat.

Once it is made there is no shifting this seat, so with this in mind take a chair (or two) to the place you intend to make the seat and sit down for a while. Ask yourself what you are going to look at when you sit there. Are you in shade or sun? Is there a path leading there? When you are quite sure you have got the siting right, decide if you want to sit alone, or whether perhaps two seats would be better.

Don't expect the appearance of the seat to be too orderly; its look should be natural. And don't worry if the odd withy cracks or splits or if you have small gaps in your weaving; this is also part of the charm. Have patience when you are weaving the seat, especially if it is your first attempt. It isn't difficult, but your skill will improve as you practise. Never try to re-weave a withy; if you must take it out, throw it away and start with a fresh one.

Shopping list

17 willow uprights, approximately 2–3cm (1in) diameter
2 bundles of green willow withies
Geotextile membrane to line seat, about 1.6m (5½ft) square
2 x 80-litre (40lb) bags of compost
Bag of horticultural grit
12 camomile plants; choose *C. nobile* 'Treneague'

Tools & equipment

1 garden cane
Surveyor's tape
Line marker paint
Metal spike and hammer, if ground is hard
Gardening gloves
Secateurs
Trowel

1 With the garden cane mark the centre of where your chair will be. Hook the surveyor's tape to the cane, measure a radius of 30cm (12in) and use the line marker paint to mark out on the ground a circle of 60cm (24in) diameter.

2 Make a mark every 10cm (4in) around the circle for the upright willow posts. Push the willow uprights into the ground until about 30cm (12in) is buried. If the ground is particularly hard you may have to use the metal spike to make a guide hole. Don't worry if you hit a stone; this stage does not need to be precise.

3 Once all the uprights are in you can begin to weave with the withies. Wear gloves, as you will find it hard on your hands. I find it most useful to wear a glove on one hand only

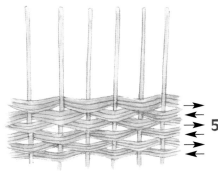

3 withies in each row woven left to right then the next row right to left

so I have one free for the fiddly ends. Weave the withies in and out of the uprights, keeping each length as neat as possible. When one runs out start the next one so it overlaps. When you have a few rows in place push down hard on the withies to compact them together. Don't worry if they seem loose; as they dry out the structure will stiffen up. Don't cut off any ends until later.

4 As you reach the level of the seat, at about 50cm (20in), do a final check for orientation – after this point it won't be possible to change your mind. Make sure that the last withy to go round does not end at the front of the seat, so that it looks neat and tidy. Cut off the uprights at the front of the seat and continue weaving just around the back of the seat. Loop some of the withies into the seat for strength and leave gaps in the back as illustrated. You can use your own artistic eye here. I prefer to leave some of the upright showing but it is up to you.

5 Trim off any of the upright ends that are too tall, getting a nice even curve to the back of the seat. Tuck in any ends that stick out or if necessary cut them off.

6 Line the seat with the geotextile membrane. This is just to help retain the compost if you have left any large gaps in the weaving. Then fill with a mixture of compost and grit. Press down the compost at regular intervals to eliminate any air pockets.

7 Plant the camomile at about 15cm (6in) intervals, putting plants right up to the front of the seat so they appear to spill over the edge. Water well. Don't sit down until the plants have had time to settle in. They should knit together to form a scented cushion and all you need do is trim with shears in late summer.

One Weekend Projects

WILDFLOWER BORDER

The wildflower border is one of my favourite projects. It can inject a natural element into a scheme and re-introduces us to flowers that are becoming less common in these days of contrived, cultivated blooms. If you only have room to devote a border to this project then you will still get immense pleasure from it, but to devote your entire lawn area will open up a whole new world of gardening. You may never want to mow again.

It is hard to resist the allure of a meadow in full flower. As a bonus, the thick grasses are home to mice and insects, and birds will feast on the seeds. You will find it a lot lower in maintenance than traditional herbaceous planting schemes, but if you are the type of gardener who likes to manicure and clip, this project is not for you.

The object of the exercise is to make the meadow look as if it has grown there by itself. Meadows are perfect if you have an area of garden that is particularly unfertile, stony or where the usual border plants need so much love and care lavishing on them that you have given up altogether. This is the reason that I suggest removing some of the good topsoil from the area to reduce the fertility of the border. Wildflowers won't thank you for any luxuries. This meadow will need a site with a good level of sunlight – a hot corner of the garden where other plants bake will do well.

A flowering meadow is at its height in the summer, but to increase the seasonal interest I have also recommended narcissi for spring colour (smaller, more delicate naturalistic varieties are better suited here), and autumn crocuses to give a good display of lavender-blue heads later in the year.

1. Remove all weeds from the area, being especially careful to rid the bed completely of perennial pests such as dock, ground elder and dandelion. They are more aggressive plants than the wildflowers and will re-colonize if you don't remove them now.

2. Remove the top layer of good topsoil and use it elsewhere in the garden. Break down the remaining soil with a border fork, then rake it gently to remove any large stones or clods of earth. Tread over the area doing the 'penguin walk' (short shuffling steps from one foot to another) to flatten the area and create a stable surface.

3. Gently rake over the area one final time. The earth should be firm, without air pockets but with a loose surface.

4. Scatter the crocus and narcissi bulbs over the area. Do this by gently tossing the bulbs to allow them to fall in a natural pattern. Plant each bulb where it falls, at a depth of 2–3 times its own height.

5. Mix the meadow grass seed with the same amount of dry sand. This will make it easier to distribute and clearer to see where you have already sown. The amount of seed per square metre or square yard will be advised on the box.

6. Rake very lightly over the area. Don't try to bury all the seeds; just gently mix them with the soil. You will now need to keep birds off the seeds. Tie strips of aluminium foil to garden canes to keep them at bay, and if you also need to deter cats spike the ground with a few more canes.

   You may be able to buy the wildflowers as plants rather than seed. If so, you will need to follow the instructions in exactly the same way but plant your wildflowers before you scatter the grass seed.

Maintenance

Mow your meadow in mid- to late spring, with the blades of the lawn-mower set at high. Don't forget to use the collection box to stop the clippings falling on the border. Mow again at the end of the summer, once again with the mower on a high setting.

Shopping list

Grass seeds, to include *Festuca* (fescues) and *Agrostis* (bents)
Bucket of fine dry sand
Seeds or plants of:
Campanula glomerata (bellflower)
Galium verum (lady's bedstraw)
Knautia arvensis (field scabious)
Leucanthemum vulgare (ox-eye daisy)
Lychnis flos-cuculi (ragged Robin)
Bulbs of:
Crocus speciosus (autumn crocus)
Narcissus pseudonarcissus

Tools & equipment

Rake
Spade
Wheelbarrow
Border fork
Garden canes
Aluminium foil

Tip

Most of us do not have room for a whole field of nodding grasses and delicate flowers. Perhaps divide the space with an organic curved line and mow only one side.

✿ Planting Variations

The plants I have listed above are just a few possibilities. Look to see what grows wild locally, or keep your eyes open for inspiration on country walks or even while browsing through magazines. Cowslips (*Primula veris*) and lady's smock (*Cardamine pratensis*) will both thrive in damper conditions and give pretty, delicate colour in spring, while musk mallow (*Malva moschata*), cornflower (*Centaurea cyanus*) and tansy (*Tanacetum vulgare*) are all robust enough to stand up to tough grasses.

A FORMAL LAWN

One of the most valuable and interesting features in your garden may also be the least esteemed and the most neglected. The humble lawn is so often overlooked in favour of more glamorous and dynamic projects, but this is a big mistake, for a clearly defined carpet of rich, close-knit green will enhance your garden, set off other features to advantage and be a year-round pleasure.

The shape of most domestic lawns can best be described as moth-eaten, the original outline eroded by years of random border expansion. The re-shaping of your lawn will bring about the most startling transformation. Far from being predictable and ordinary, a simple geometric shape in a swathe of emerald green can be the first building block in your overall garden design. Nor is a formal lawn biased towards a particular style of garden – a perfect square of turf will complement a modern minimalist scheme just as well as an exuberance of traditional borders.

A formal lawn should be accurately laid out. Choose a simple, symmetrical shape and line up a square or rectangle with the flat plane of the house; a circle will look best if the centre point is aligned with an important vista or doorway. The neat edges, kept in place by an edging line, will enable the shape to remain clear and true, removing the temptation to 'chew' the edge and lose the effect. When planning the dimensions of your lawn, allow enough space around it to accommodate paths and borders. Flower borders should aim for a minimum width of 1m (3ft); any less than this and the plants will soon become cramped.

1 Mow the lawn before starting. Using the garden canes, roughly mark out the shape and size of lawn you require.

For a square or oblong lawn

2 Mark out the edge that is parallel to the house or wall that you are aligning the lawn with. Do this by measuring from the wall to your line and check the measurement at several points, or, as in the illustration, along an existing patio.

3 To ensure your corners are right angles, measure out a 3, 4, 5 triangle at either corner (see page 132). Draw in these lines with the marker paint and then join their two ends to complete the box. A useful final check to ensure you have a rectangle and not a parallelogram is to measure the two diagonals: they should be the same length.

4 Now you have the lawn marked out, take a measurement around the perimeter. This will give you the total length of timber edge board you need to buy.

5 Cut along the marked lines using the half moon or sharp spade; put a board on the grass to stand on and also to use as a straight line guide.

6 Cut the timber stakes into 30cm (1ft) lengths and make a point at one end of each length with the wood chisel. Make the point as

Shopping list

I have not given the number of lengths of timber needed for this feature because it will depend on the size of your lawn. Once you have completed step 4 you can measure the outline of your shape and gauge the approximate amount of timber you will require.

Tanalized 10cm (4in) timber edge boards, 2m (6½ft) long
Tanalized 2 x 2cm (¾ x ¾in) timber lengths, 2m (6½ft) long

Tools & equipment

A couple of dozen garden canes
Surveyor's tape
Line marker paint
Half-moon edge cutter or small flat spade
Wood saw
Wood chisel
Wooden mallet
Trowel

4   5

90°

3

cane

Tip

To achieve the right effect, the grass will need to be in good condition. Grass is a remarkably resilient plant, and even a mossy, weedy lawn with bare patches can be brought back to life with a little tender loving care. Where your lawn is sited may well be pre-determined, but do make sure that it is an area of good light levels; lawns will not thrive in deep shade

Above This fabulously formal lawn is complemented by the terracotta terrace and edge.

Right A soft circle is just right for a corner of this plot, the small curved bench echoing the theme

even as possible so that the stake can easily be knocked in without fear of twisting.

7   Place the tanalized timber edge boards upright along the newly cut lawn edge so that the top of the timber is very slightly below the level of the lawn. You may have to

use the trowel to make a gully to push the board into. Knock the timber stakes into the ground approximately every 50cm (18in) or so, so that they hold the board tightly against the lawn edge. Cut off the tops of the stakes so that they are flush with the edging timbers.

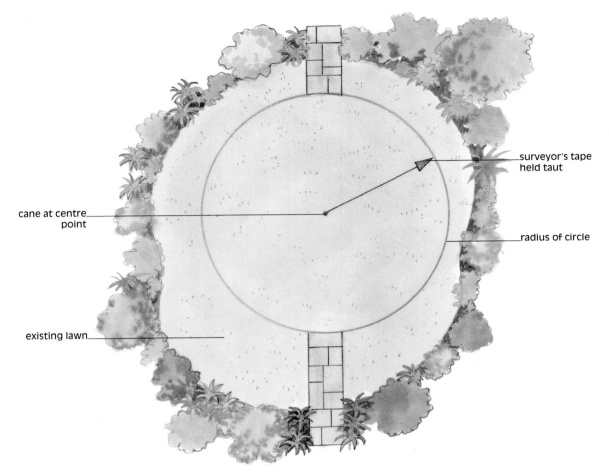

cane at centre point

surveyor's tape held taut

radius of circle

existing lawn

Drawing out a circular lawn

The most common shape for a formal lawn is square, but a circular lawn also works well in many situations. The important thing to remember is to be accurate; never mark it out by eye.

1 Push a cane into the centre point of your circle. Hook on the end of the surveyor's tape, hold the tape taut at the desired radius for your circle and scribe it using the line marker paint.

2 Cut along the marked line as in step 5 on page 57. You can't use a board to help guide you, but stand on a short board to spread your weight and to avoid making a mess of the lawn.

3 The rest of the process is the same as for a square lawn, except that the edging boards will have to be

encouraged to curve. To do this, lay the edging boards down flat and make cuts every 5cm (2in) to a depth of approximately 5mm (¼in). If you are making a very small lawn with a tight curve you may have to make more frequent cuts. The timber will now bend easily. The boards are held in place in just the same way, but with a small circle you may need to place the stakes closer together.

Maintenance

During the summer use a liquid weed and feed preparation according to the manufacturer's instructions. When you mow, keep the blades on a high setting and remove any grass clippings unless you are a very regular mower, in which case you can leave them on the lawn. Rake the area in spring and autumn to remove any thatch, which is a build-up of dead material and moss.

❖ **Project Links**

A small formal lawn will need equally ordered borders. In a tiny garden it is nice to use plants of a similar colour to create a themed border (see pages 70–72).

A finishing touch to complement the elegance of the lawn would be obelisks (see pages 80–83). Two at the far end of the garden or one in each corner would add height and permanent structure, and during the winter, when the plants are not as prolific, they will give a sculptural element to your garden.

OAK BENCH

Every garden, no matter how small, should have at least one seat, somewhere to regard the garden from a lower vantage point and where you can rest with a cup of tea after a day's hard horticultural labour. This bench is the simplest type of seat, constructed from three pieces of oak. It is well within the abilities of most practically minded gardeners, although you may find it useful to ask a friend to help with the assembly as the proportions make it rather heavy.

Tip

Your bench will need a firm base to stand on, but this need not be a paved area. If you want to set it in grass (it looks particularly good nestled in a meadow), then two slabs set at lawn level will provide a sturdy base. Use a spirit level to make sure that the slabs are level or you will find that the bench rocks, possibly dangerous with a feature as heavy as this.

There are endless possibilities to make variations on the theme of this bench. It would lend itself to doubling in length, although you may need to add an extra leg in the middle, or equally you can reduce it in size and treat it as one seat in a set. Before embarking on the construction, re-read Seating in Design Essentials (page 18) and consider where in the garden it would best be set.

The wood for the bench will be easily available from your local timber yard. If you ask very nicely they may also cut the legs to size for you. When a seat is made from a material as beautiful as oak it is a crime to stain or paint it and quite unnecessary from the point of preservation. Oak will survive outside for many years, fading with the elements to a beautiful grey-silver colour. At first it may seem the perfect seat for a natural woodland setting but because of its elegant simplicity I think it would also work in a minimal scheme, taking on sculptural properties when uncluttered by plants and other features. If you have difficulty locating oak you can use a treated softwood, although you will lose the depth of grain and subtle natural colour.

Shopping list

1 piece of green oak 30 x 30cm and 2m long (1 x 1ft and 6–6½ft long)
2 steel bolts 30cm (12in) long x 15mm (½in) diameter

Tools & equipment

Soft pencil
Rule
Right-angle rule
Wood saw
Silicone spray
25mm (1in) chisel
Hammer/mallet
Electric drill
15mm (½in) drill bit
25mm (1in) drill bit
Socket set with 15mm (½in) socket

1   Draw two pencil lines 30cm (12in) in from each end of the oak piece. Using the right-angle rule, draw the line all the way around the wood so there is a guide line on every side.

2   Saw along the guide lines. Try to use the entire length of your blade and watch the guide lines carefully. Go slowly – it is a very large lump of wood. If your saw sticks, spray the blade with silicone to help it slide more easily. The two 30cm (12in) cubes you have sawn off will be used to form the legs of the bench and the remaining long piece will be the seat.

3   Choose which will be the underside of the seat and on that side draw a straight pencil line 20cm (8in) from one end of the oak and a second line 50cm (20in) from the end, to give you two parallel lines 30cm (12in) apart. Using the right-angle rule, continue these lines down the front and back of the seat to a length of 15cm (6in). Join the ends of these lines to form a rectangle.

When you remove the wood within the area you have drawn you will have a recess for a leg to fit into.

4   To remove the waste wood, work with the underside of the seat uppermost. Saw carefully down the two parallel lines at 20 and 50cm (8 and 20in) to a depth of 15cm (6in), following the pencil guide lines. Make several more cuts at random in parallel within the two guide lines. Use a chisel to remove all the waste wood from the recess, leaving a clean U-shaped gully.

Repeat steps 3 and 4 for the other end of the bench.

5   Place the seat over the two legs. The legs should fit snugly into their recesses in the seat.

6   Make two pencil marks on the top of the bench 30cm (12in) in from each end and 15cm (6in) in from either side. Using the 25mm (1in) drill bit, make a hole approximately 2cm (¾in) deep.

7   In the same hole use the 15mm (½in) drill bit to drill a hole through the seat and into the leg to a depth of 20cm (8in). Using the socket insert the bolt into the hole and tighten.

Repeat steps 6 and 7 for the second leg.

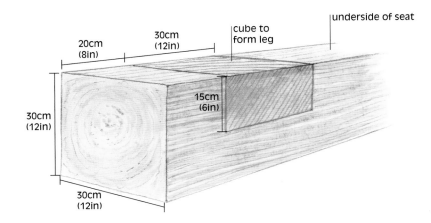

20cm (8in)
30cm (12in)
cube to form leg
underside of seat
15cm (6in)
30cm (12in)
30cm (12in)

WATER FEATURE FOR A SMALL GARDEN

Water can be the very heart of a garden design, but it can also be an expensive feature, and a daunting one to install, especially for new gardeners. This water feature is the simplest of all ideas. It needs no pump, and therefore no electricity, and will require only a clear-up twice a year in spring and autumn. In return you will get an amazing array of insects and animal life visiting your garden, not to mention fantastic blooms from the water lily and sparkling reflections on a sunny day.

This pool's most appealing quality is its simplicity – to overplant it would ruin the elegant lines. The pygmy water lily is the most exquisite choice for a small, simple water feature such as this, but whichever type of plants you choose you will need to police growth vigilantly, keeping them within the area in which they were planted.

A worry about static water is stagnation. The plants turn the water into a living, breathing feature and if you get the right balance should keep away any nasty green slime.

Although this is only a small pond, it is not suitable for a garden where there are young children. There is more than enough water to drown in and it is just too tempting for them to stay away, even when warned.

1 Mark out two concentric circles, one the diameter of your water tank and one about 20cm (8in) wider. Do this by putting a garden cane at the centre of where you want your pond. Attach the end of the surveyor's tape to the cane and then scribe the two circles with the tape pulled taut.

2 Dig out the inner circle to a depth of 2cm (1in) deeper than your tank and the second circle to a depth of 2cm (1in) deeper than your slate – this will form a shelf for the slate. Use the tank as a guide by regularly trying it in the hole. It needs to fit snugly so it doesn't move around. Also make sure you remove any

rocks or sharp rubble that project into the hole.

3 Scatter about 2cm (1in) of sand into the bottom of the hole so that the tank has a firm base on which to rest. Put the tank into the hole. It is essential that the tank is perfectly level or the water level will not be right. Use your spirit level to check.

4 Put a layer of sand 2–3cm (1in) deep on the 'shelf' around the tank. Don't worry about getting sand into the tank; it is inevitable at this point. Start to lay the slates on edge around the water tank. You will need to stand back every few

Shopping list

Circular plastic header tank
Sand
Blue slate – broken slates are perfect
Washed gravel (any gauge)
2 pieces of steel air-conditioning pipe the same length as the depth of the tank. One should be about two-thirds the diameter of the tank, the other about one-third the diameter.
Zebra grass (*Miscanthus sinensis* 'Zebrinus')
Pygmy water lily (*Nymphaea* 'Pygmaea Helvola')

Tools & equipment

Surveyor's tape
Garden cane
Line marker paint
Spade
Spirit level
Brick guillotine that closes completely
Rubber mallet

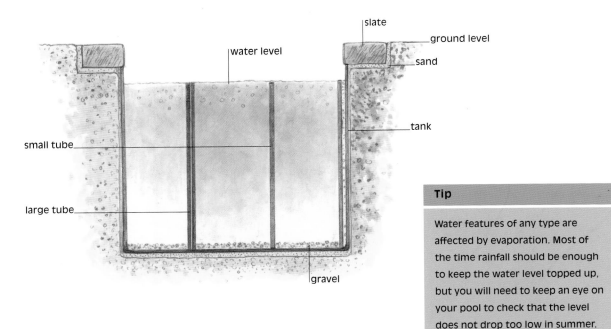

small tube
large tube
water level
slate
ground level
sand
tank
gravel

Tip

Water features of any type are affected by evaporation. Most of the time rainfall should be enough to keep the water level topped up, but you will need to keep an eye on your pool to check that the level does not drop too low in summer.

✿ Planting Variations

As the pool is entirely flat the vertical element of planting is essential to add structure and form. I am particularly fond of the zebra grass but you could try using *Typha minima*, the dwarf bulrush. Don't be tempted by the ordinary varieties; they will grow much too large in a very short space of time; only the *minima* is small enough for this situation. Other suitable vertical plants to consider are *Cyperus longus*, which has an interesting umbrella shape, or *Iris pseudacorus*, which will introduce yellow blooms to the scheme while maintaining height.

Above *Iris pseudacorus*.

Ordinary water lilies are also far too rampant. If you really need an alternative, try *Caltha palustris*, the yellow kingcup.

Remember to check that each plant is at the depth it requires; this should be on the pot containing the plant. You can adjust this by raising or lowering the gravel in the tank.

Left *Nymphaea pigmaea* 'Helvola'.

slates to make sure that they point towards the centre of the circle and check that they are level with the surrounding earth. You can use the brick guillotine to cut any slates that are too large. When you have gone all the way round, the slates should be tightly packed on the inner circle. You can then add smaller slates on the outside of the circle, banging them in gently with

Right *Miscanthus sinensis* 'Zebrinus'.

the rubber mallet. When you have gone all the way round, the slates should be stable, each one held in place by the one either side.

5   Now clean out any sand that has fallen in and put a small layer of gravel in the bottom of the tank. Then put the larger diameter of the two pipes into the tank and settle it into the gravel so that it touches one side of the slate edge. Put some more gravel on the outside of the pipe to bed it in. Now put the smaller pipe into the larger one so that it is in the centre of the tank. Fill the small pipe with a little more gravel.

6   Fill the tank with water and allow it to settle.

7   Plant the zebra grass in the central pipe and the water lily in the outer pond. Make sure that they are in the correct depth of water – you can stand them on more gravel or an engineering brick bedded in the gravel if you need to raise them.

DECORATIVE SCREEN

One of the simplest ways to add excitement and a sense of discovery to a garden, however small it might be, is a dividing screen that creates smaller areas or rooms. This does not necessarily mean creating a solid, impermeable dividing wall – a screen that you can see over or through can have the same effect, intriguing visitors and enticing them to explore your garden.

For one 2m (6½ft) screen:
2 tanalized 10 x 10cm (4 x 4in)
    timber uprights, 2.4m (8ft)
    long
2 wooden post finials
2 bags of post mix
10 turn buckles and grips
2 tanalized 20 x 2cm (8 x ¾in)
    timber boards, 2m (6½ft) long
12 zinc-plated screws, 3.5cm
    (1½in) long
Reel of steel wire
3 x 80-litre (40lb) bags of good-
    quality compost
4 ivy plants (*Hedera helix*)

Tools & equipment

Spade
Soft pencil
Spirit level
Electric drill with screwdriver
    fitting
Right-angle rule
Soft garden string

With this simple but effective design, it might be the woven wire pattern that is the screen, or the ivy climbing along it: the choice is entirely yours. Ivy, which has many pretty variations, will provide colour all year round and if pruned regularly will take exactly to the shape of the wire to produce a geometric patterned green wall.

A screen can also help with privacy. You may have a terrace that is overlooked by other houses, but to screen it completely might make the area claustrophobic and give too much shade. A permeable screen like this will provide enough seclusion for the impression of privacy without giving the feeling that you are blocked in.

This screen is constructed as a single unit, but it would be possible to add several units together to create a larger screen, or to construct two screens at right angles to make a secret corner.

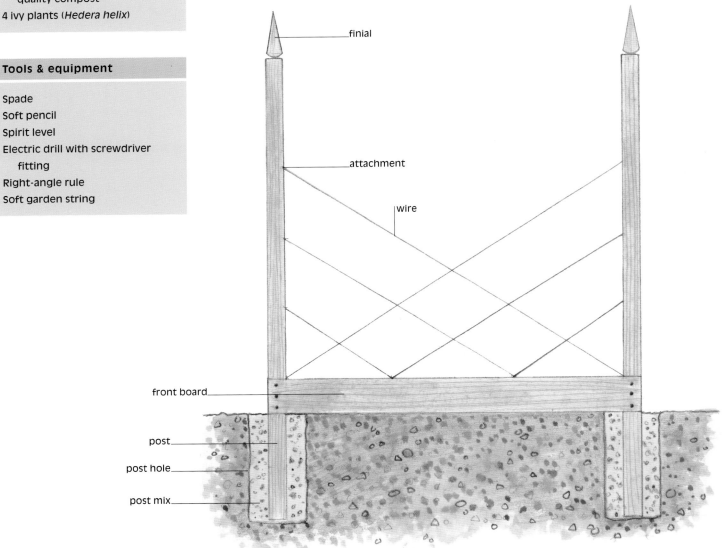

finial

attachment

wire

front board

post

post hole

post mix

1 Dig two post holes 60cm (24in) deep and 30cm (12in) wide, with their centres 2m (6½ft) apart.

2 Measure 60cm (24in) from the bottom end of each upright and run a pencil mark around the post: this is where the ground level will be. Screw the finials in place on the top of the uprights.

3 Put one upright in each hole. Set the posts in place with post mix, ensuring that 1.8m (6ft) of the post shows above ground and that their centres are exactly 2m (6½ft) apart. Use the spirit level to check that they are vertical. You might have to attach temporary support timbers to hold the posts upright while the post mix sets.

4 Once the posts are set firm, drill four pilot holes on the internal face of each upright, the first one 20cm (8in) from the ground, then three more at 40cm (16in) spacing. Screw in a turn buckle and grip attachment at each hole.

5 Next, attach the two boards to the uprights to form bottom panels, using three screws in a line to hold each board end.

6 Drill two pilot holes at equidistant points in the top edge of the front board. Do this carefully as the boards can very easily be split. Then screw in the two final turn buckles and grips.

7 Run the steel wire to join the top left turn buckle with the bottom right, and the top right with the bottom left. Then join up the others to make a pattern of diagonals, as shown opposite.

8 The two bottom boards have created a planter. Fill this with compost and plant the ivies, one at each point where the wires are attached to the planter edge. Tie in the ivy tendrils with string, so that they follow the wire form.

✿ Planting Variations

If your main concern is privacy during the summer months and you need a fast-growing block of startling foliage, substitute golden hop, *Humulus lupulus* 'Aureus'. This climber will have no respect for your carefully placed wires but will cover them over in a matter of months, giving a lime-green bank of foliage with only the top outline showing. The down side of hop is that it is deciduous, so in winter you will have a tangle of brown stems. However, I leave these on show in my own garden. I find the twisted stems have a beauty all of their own, especially when covered with frost or dew. Cut down to the base in spring and the plant will shoot with new vigour, covering the screen in double quick time with larger, more vibrant foliage, and once it is well established you will also get sprays of hops in autumn.

Above *Humulus lupulus* 'Aureus'.

Left *Hedera helix* 'Astin'.

CHILDREN'S WIGWAM

This project can easily be constructed within one weekend but the best part is that it will look better and better as each month passes. It is tempting to put children's play items as far away as possible and preferably out of sight, but small children will prefer to play near to the safety of the house and this wigwam is so great-looking it merits a position in full view.

The wigwam is a living structure, so it will need a site where the willow withies will have their feet in the earth. Willow will grow just about anywhere but it prefers an area with a good moisture level. A lawn area would be fine, as would a border or uncultivated corner of the garden.

This is a project for mid-autumn to early spring. This is the time that the willow withies will be cut; willow that is available during the summer months is brown and has been cut and bundled for some time and therefore it will not grow. Don't be fooled by the fact that willow withies have no roots. If you gently scrape the stems you will see there is a green layer, showing you that they are alive and will start to produce roots as soon as they hit the earth. During the growing season of spring to late summer, the willow will produce lots of shoots from the upright stems. It is entirely up to you to decide which shoots you are going to remove and which ones you will tuck into the uprights to make a living green haven.

1 Mark out the circle for the wigwam by placing the cane, with the surveyor's tape hooked on, at the centre of the site. Pull the tape taut and scribe a circle with the marker paint. The radius of the circle should be 75cm (2½ft) giving you a diameter of 1.5m (5ft).

2 Decide which way you would like the entrance to face and mark a gap 60cm (2ft) wide along the circle. Draw two parallel lines out from these marks to create an entrance tunnel. Make the tunnel 1m (3ft) long.

3 On the circular line hammer the metal spike into the ground every 20cm (8in) and then push a willow withy into the hole to a depth of about 20–30cm (8–12in). You may not need the spike if the ground is soft. Don't forget to leave a gap for the entrance, and then insert withies along the lines of the tunnel entrance as well.

4 Using the soft string, cross the tops of the withies over the entrance and tie them together in pairs to create a tunnel.

5 Cover the ground inside the wigwam and tunnel with the geotextile membrane and then with a layer of bark chippings.

Place the two tree-trunk offcuts inside the wigwam as seats.

6 Draw the tops of the circle of withies together to form the wigwam itself. You may find it easier to collect every other withy in a bunch and tie these together first, then join the remaining ones to the first bunch.

7 Dig planting holes, one either side of the tunnel entrance and one at the back of the wigwam. Plant the vines (*Vitis vinifera* 'Purpurea') and tie them in to the willow uprights using soft string.

Tip

You will need to spend a little time maintaining the wigwam if it is to retain its shape, but this is a good opportunity to get the children interested in gardening. While you are pruning and weaving, keep stepping back to view the wigwam from a distance. Most of all, don't be afraid to cut back; it is highly unlikely that you will kill the willow through over-enthusiastic pruning. Do keep the top of the wigwam in check unless you want it to reach colossal proportions.

Shopping list

2 bundles of cut green willow

3 *Vitis vinifera* 'Purpurea'

Geotextile membrane, approximately 3sq m (30sq ft)

3 x 80-litre (40lb) bags of bark chippings

2 tree-trunk offcuts, about 30cm (1ft) high, for seats

Tools & equipment

Surveyor's tape

Garden cane

Line marker paint

Metal spike or tent peg at least 30cm (12in) long

Hammer

Soft string

Spade

✿ Planting Variations

None of the alternative plants for weaving is as good as willow. Hazel (*Corylus*) is the best of them, but hazel whips are usually less readily available and several times more expensive. Hazel is also slower-growing than willow and less easy to work with.

You can, however, change the climbers that are scrambling over the wigwam, or leave them out altogether – they certainly aren't necessary to hold the structure together. Children are generally no respecters of plant life, especially during a good game, so whatever you choose will have to be sturdy.

❖ Project Links

This wigwam would make a fun centrepiece for the paving maze (see page 126). Unless you have plenty of room to devote to a large maze, you may need to make the wigwam a little smaller, especially as once it starts to grow it will take up more space than when it is first planted. Reducing the radius by about 10cm (4in) should be enough. You will have to omit the entrance tunnel. Don't forget to make sure that the route through the maze finishes at the wigwam's entrance.

COLOUR-THEMING A BORDER

When your garden, or just one border, has a colour theme, it contributes a look of unity and order. Some might say it is boring to choose only one colour, but this type of design works best if you use the enormous range of tones and hues that you find within a single colour family, allowing you to use several colours that blend so perfectly it is an exercise in harmony.

The plants for this project are for a blue border but they use shades from deep purple through to pale powder-blue, along with purple foliage plants enhanced by silver-leaved plants giving a contrast colour to the display. It is often exciting to throw in a contrasting colour with the harmonious mix. An orange foxtail lily (*Eremurus*) adrift in this sea of blue would have a stunning starring role, as opposed to being lost in a range of plants in toning colours.

You may not be starting from scratch with this border. If you have a planted area that is looking a little uncoordinated, take careful notes of the plants you have and try to choose your theme to harmonize with them. On the other hand, be prepared to sacrifice a large established plant if it just won't match your new scheme.

You can follow whatever colour theme is to your taste, but take into account the hard landscape materials that will be nearby, including your house if it forms part of the backdrop. When it comes to plants there are thousands of options, so consider the soil type and situation you are offering and choose your plants accordingly.

1 Dig over your border. If it is an existing site, remove all of the plants that are already there and set them carefully to one side. If the border includes very large shrubs then consider each one carefully before you remove it. A plant that is very large will not transplant easily, but there is no point in leaving it just because it is big if it doesn't go with your chosen theme.

2 Spread a layer of well-rotted manure over the border and lightly fork it in.

3 Arrange all the plants on the border to see how they work together. The ceanothus is a large, quite dense shrub and will need to go at the rear of the border. Tall perennials that keep their structure and interest all year round with seedheads, such as fennel, eryngium and echinops, need to go towards the rear, with the smaller perennials towards the front. The climbers can go at the very back of the border if there is a fence to support them or towards the middle of the border on a willow obelisk.

4 Once you are happy with the plants' positions, plant them with a handful of fertilizer granules in each hole and don't forget to

Shopping list

Slow-release fertilizer
Well-rotted manure
Willow obelisk
Bark chipping mulch

Plants for a blue theme:
SHRUBS:
Ceanothus arboreus 'Burkwoodii'

PERENNIALS AND BULBS:
Artemisia 'Powis Castle'
Camassia quamash
Catananche caerulea 'Major'
Echinops ritro 'Veitch's Blue'
Eryngium giganteum
Foeniculum vulgare
    'Purpurascens' (purple fennel)
Lavandula angustifolia 'Hidcote'
Muscari
Nepeta 'Six Hills Giant' (catmint)
Salvia officinalis 'Purpurea'
    (purple sage)

CLIMBERS:
Clematis alpina 'Frances Rivis'
Solanum crispum

Tools & equipment

Border spade
Border fork
Trowel

Left to right
Muscari latifolium,
Echinops ritro
'Veitch's Blue',
Eryngium
giganteum.

✿ Planting Variations

Plants for a white theme

SHRUBS:

Deutzia gracilis

Philadelphus 'Virginal'

Rosa 'Iceberg'

PERENNIALS AND BULBS:

Artemisia

Digitalis purpurea 'Alba' (white foxgloves)

Galanthus nivalis (snowdrops)

Papaver orientale 'Perry's White'

white tulips, such as *Tulipa* 'White Dream'

Zantedeschia aethiopica 'Crowborough'

CLIMBERS:

Jasminum officinale (summer jasmine)

Lathyrus latifolius 'Albus' (sweet pea)

Plants for a pink theme

SHRUBS:

a pink rose

Viburnum x *bodnantense* 'Dawn'

Weigela florida

PERENNIALS AND BULBS:

Left *Allium hollandicum*.

Allium hollandicum

Anemone japonica

Colchicum speciosum (autumn crocus)

Digitalis purpurea (foxgloves)

Geranium endressii

Heuchera micrantha 'Palace Purple'

Penstemon 'Apple Blossom'

Physostegia virginiana

CLIMBERS:

Clematis 'Nelly Moser'

Wisteria sinensis

water them, even if it has been raining recently.

5 Spread a thick layer of bark mulch over the soil between the plants; this will help suppress weeds and retain moisture.

Below *Papaver orientale* 'Perry's White'.   **Right** *Penstemon* 'Apple Blossom'.

Tip

Try to make your border a minimum of 1m (3ft) wide. It is tempting to make borders narrow, but perennials quickly double in size and you will find that they overtake a small area. If you have room for a border that is 2m (6ft) or more wide, all the better. A stepping stone or two placed in between the plants will give access for maintenance.

Always plant your perennials in groups of odd number; they will appear as one drift and not as individual plants. Bulbs should be planted in drifts as naturally as possible, even directly under the canopy of perennial leaves where they will bloom through the other plants.

LOW-MAINTENANCE COURTYARD

'I want a garden but I don't have time to look after it' is a familiar cry. There is no such thing as a no-maintenance garden, but low-maintenance doesn't mean low-style or low-interest. This project is designed for quite a small area, which could either be the entire plot or a quiet corner you have chosen. The planting is restrained, and tactile features such as the dinosaur-egg cobbles and a bench or sculpture complete the elegant design.

*I haven't specified amounts for
this project because it can be
applied to so many spaces. Use
my directions as a guide. You will
find local building suppliers very
helpful when it comes to
calculating gravel and membrane
amounts – just take the
measurements with you.*

Geotextile membrane, enough
    to cover the area you are
    working on
Pea gravel – 0.5 tonne per square
    metre or square yard of
    courtyard
Specimen-size plants (in at least
    10-litre [5lb] pots) of
    *Phyllostachys nigra,
    Ophiopogon planiscapus*
    'Nigrescens', *Phormium tenax*
Good-quality compost
Slow-release fertilizer granules
Extra-large 'dinosaur-egg'
    cobbles
Seat or bench

Tools & equipment

Spade
Wheelbarrow
Rake
Craft knife

Tip

If your courtyard has solid
boundaries such as walls or fences,
you could consider painting them.
White would be too stark, but a pale
cream would act as a very effective
foil for the dark stems of the
bamboo and the striking red leaves
of the phormium.

In this minimalist plan, 'less is more', and plants have been kept to only a very few types. This means that each must be hard-working, and so that the courtyard looks as good in winter as summer my choices are all evergreen. The bamboo makes a wonderful rattling sound when moved by the wind. The colour of its stems is picked up by the black, grass-like leaves of the ophiopogon, while the deep red phormium adds a stunning silhouette of sword-like leaves. All these plants require minimum maintenance, occasional trimming of dead leaves and a little food two or three times a year. As there are so few plants to buy, I do urge you to go for large specimens. Of course bigger plants are more expensive, but the impact they will provide will justify the cost and you won't need so many.

Geotextile membrane will help keep maintenance to a minimum. It allows moisture to pass through into the earth but doesn't allow weeds to grow up through it. Along with the gravel it will keep moisture near the roots of the plants, so reducing the need to water.

1 Clear the area completely of any free-standing objects. Dig up and dispose of any grass or plants.

2 Remove any existing courtyard surface to 5cm (2in) below the finished level. Rake the surface level and tread it down to compact the earth. If you are going to paint your boundaries, do it now.

3 Cut the geotextile membrane to the size of your courtyard and lay it on top of the compacted earth. Weigh it down with a few stones.

4 Spread a layer of pea gravel over the membrane to a depth of 5cm (2in) until the courtyard is completely covered.

5 Arrange plants in the courtyard in groups of three or five, not too close together. Also decide where your seat will go. You could position it to give you a good view of the courtyard or perhaps nestle it among the plants for seclusion. When you are happy with the arrangement, move the seat out of the way and rake back the gravel under each plant (using the back of the rake so as not to rip the membrane). With the craft knife, cut a cross in the membrane where each plant is to go and fold back the edges of the cross.

6 Dig a large planting pit for each plant, at least twice the size of the pot that it is in. Fill the hole with compost and a handful of slow-release fertilizer granules and plant into it, firming the plant in well.

7 Water each plant and then carefully replace the geotextile membrane and re-cover with the gravel so that the plant appears to spring from the ground.

8 Arrange the large cobbles in groups among the planting. Groups of odd numbers such as three, five or seven often work best visually. You may have to do this several times to get it right. Finally, put your seat back in place.

✿ Planting Variations

For a slightly more orderly and formal look to the courtyard you could use large bushes of clipped box (*Buxus sempervirens*), preferably in pyramid form. Add to this some smaller spheres of box and, for just a touch of understated colour, tall white spikes of foxtail lily (*Eremurus himalaicus*) that can emerge from a carpet of *Soleirolia soleirolii* (mind-your-own-business).

❖ Project Links

A curving pergola (see page 112) would make an excellent additional feature to a low-maintenance garden without adding hugely to its upkeep. Ornate deciduous flowering climbers adorning the uprights would certainly mean more maintenance, but ivy (*Hedera helix*) will give you evergreen leaves all year round with only the minimum of clearing-up to do. Initially the plants will need support to help them cling to the uprights, but once they get established they will develop aerial roots which they will use to attach themselves to the wood.

In a small area it would be best to site the pergola right in the middle of the plot. You can then use the central circular space for dining or seating, with the pergola entrance orientated towards the most convenient doorway. If you are fortunate enough to have a larger area to design you may still wish to use the pergola as a central feature, or you could site it in one corner of the design so that it creates a walkway through an area of planting.

One Weekend Projects

Left Planting through gravel is a great low-maintenance trick, and the plants look even better with the addition of smooth boulders to act as a foil for the architectural foliage.

LIGHTING

Lighting your garden means you can enjoy it to the full on balmy summer evenings, and even from inside the house lights will turn your view of the garden from a black void into a living picture, changing with the seasons. Lighting is usually one of the more expensive and complicated projects for a garden, but these simple lighting ideas avoid both these drawbacks.

Most lights require an electricity supply which has to be installed by a qualified electrician. The beauty of solar-powered lighting is that it is as easy as opening the box and siting the light where you need it. Most solar-powered lights will have an additional plug so that you can top up the battery if there has not been enough sunlight to charge it during the day.

Using candles in the garden is one of my favourite ways to light. Their main disadvantage is that they need to be shielded from the wind or you will spend the whole evening re-lighting them. Jamjars are perfect for this – inexpensive and available in many sizes and shapes. The flickering light they give is especially good for creating atmosphere for a party.

Larger jars can line the edge of paths and terraces, or sit along the coping stones on top of walls. Hang smaller jars in trees and bushes. They will look best if you use them in numbers, but make sure that there is no foliage hanging over the top of the jar or it will scorch. Use small hooks (galvanized so they won't rust) to hang more jars from the crossbeams of pergolas and similar structures, and light up a pool by floating a wide, shallow jar on the surface of the static water.

Shopping list

Solar powered spotlights (with spikes)
Glass jamjars (empty and clean) of varying sizes, the more the better
Steel garden wire
Night light candles (tea lights)

Tools & equipment

Pliers
Torch
Taper and matches

One Weekend Projects

1 Put the solar lights on to charge. You may have to leave them overnight for their first charge.

2 Make handles for the smaller jamjars to hang from. Cut a length of steel garden wire and loop it round the top of a jamjar, just underneath the lip or screw fitting. Twist the wire around itself until it makes a tight loop, then twist the short end until it is securely fastened and neat. Make the long end of the wire into a handle and tuck the end under the loop of wire around the neck, twisting it on securely.

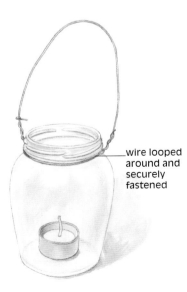

wire looped around and securely fastened

3 Repeat this with all the hanging jars and put a night light in the bottom of each one.

4 Wait until dusk! It is much easier to site your lights in the correct place if you wait until the sun is going down. You may find it useful to have a torch at the ready, just in case it takes longer than you thought to complete the job.

Spotlights need to be carefully placed or your garden will look more like a prison than a pleasure garden. If you have trees, then place a spotlight or two not far from the base of the trunk and angle the spot upwards into the canopy of the tree. The light will play on the leaves as they move, giving a surreal look. Even in winter a tree's illuminated skeleton is quite wonderful.

If you have changes in level in the garden, place spotlights either side of a step and shine the light across the rise and tread. This has a twofold use: as a practical guide to getting around the garden at night and as decorative lighting. Finally, direct spotlights onto arches, sculptures or large pots. The spot will need to be placed at least 1m (3ft) away from the features, and

make sure that the angle of the spot does not mean that it will shine into your face as you walk by.

5 Put your jamjars in place and light the candles (use a taper to reach into the jars without burning your fingers). Make sure that the paths are wide enough so that the jars won't be knocked over.

Above When a tree is lit by spotlights it takes on a sculptural quality and becomes a living picture.

It would be true to say that things are getting a little more complicated – these projects are a little more demanding in terms of your time and concentration, but then the rewards are greater.

TWO WEEKEND PROJECTS

2

Two Weekend Projects

OBELISK

The downfall of newly planted gardens is often their lack of height. Trees and shrubs can take years to achieve maturity, leaving new gardens looking very flat and uninspiring. Introduce an obelisk into the scheme, however, and you will add height, variety and a focal point without having to wait for plants to grow. A pair will stand sentinel to an entrance or either side of a path; a group of three, perhaps in varying heights, will really make an impact.

An obelisk is a tapered structure, usually of wood or metal. It can be used to support climbing plants, but if it is a thing of beauty it will stand as a garden feature on its own. In a formal scheme obelisks can punctuate a knot garden, mark the crossing of paths or 'reward' the eye at the end of a vista. Think carefully about how you position your obelisk, for this is no shrinking violet. It will draw attention to any area in which it features.

Don't be afraid of scale – however tall you were imagining, double it! Obelisks should be slender and elegant, never stubby. The minimum height is 1.5m (5ft) and, depending on the scheme of your garden, up to 3m (10ft) tall would not be out of the question. Remember, obelisks taper to a point and are semi-see-through, so, although tall, they give the sense of a delicate trellis rather than a solid block.

On a practical note, it is better if the obelisk can be pushed into the ground at least 20cm (8in), to give some anchorage. Should you decide to adorn your obelisk with a climbing plant, this will also help to anchor it to the earth.

Shopping list

To make one obelisk 1.8m (6ft) tall:

4 tanalized 5 x 5cm (2 x 2in) timber uprights, 2m (6½ft) long
13 tanalized 25mm x 5mm (1 x ¼in) laths, 2m (6½ft) long
100 zinc-plated screws, 3.5cm (1⅜in) long
1 piece of tanalized timber 12.5cm (5in) square and 2.5cm (1in) thick
1 zinc-plated screw, 7cm (2¾in) long
4 zinc-plated screws, 5cm (2in) long
1 wooden finial, ball or point
1 small can of exterior-grade undercoat
1 small can of exterior-grade satin paint

Tools & equipment

Soft pencil
Measuring tape
Wood saw
Cordless drill with screwdriver head
3.5mm (⅛in) drill bit
Line marker paint or chalk
Paintbrush

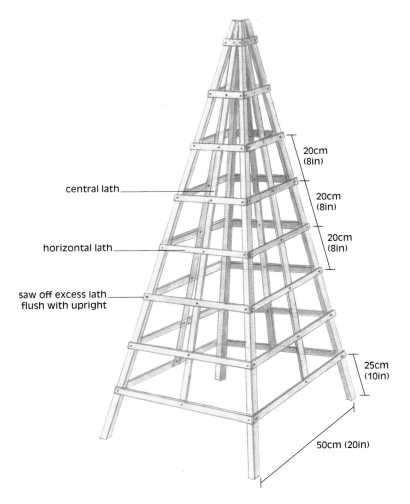

central lath

horizontal lath

saw off excess lath flush with upright

20cm (8in)

20cm (8in)

20cm (8in)

25cm (10in)

50cm (20in)

1 Place two of the timber uprights on the ground in an upside-down V-shape, touching each other at one end and with the other ends spread out to a distance of 50cm (20in) apart.

With a pencil make marks on the upright timbers at 20cm (8in) intervals, starting 25cm (10in) from the bottom of the ends that are spread apart.

2 Place a lath horizontally between the two uprights, aligning a pair of

pencil marks. Drill pilot holes and then screw through the lath into the uprights, using the smallest size of screws.

Saw off the excess lath flush with the upright. Continue to attach the laths in this way until you have a tapering ladder effect.

3 When all of the horizontal laths are in place, place a central lath down the middle of the ladder on the inside. Drill a pilot hole and screw together at every point at which the laths cross, screwing from the

Right The symmetrical placement of four powder-blue obelisks turns an ordinary plot into a stylish formal garden.

Tip

Garden obelisks are all about making a statement. They are contrived garden paraphernalia that don't pretend to be subtle or blend with the surroundings, so why not paint your obelisk a bold colour? Choose your colour carefully. Don't go for green – invariably it will be an inferior colour to the shades that nature can provide. Try instead a blue or purple shade, or, if you are feeling really bold and brave, a deep burgundy would look stunning against a green hedge. Bright colours don't look cheap if you use a rich or dark tone. Consider echoing the colour of an adjacent bed – if you have a white border scheme then a cream-coloured obelisk will highlight your design.

outside in. Don't be tempted to screw into the timber without using pilot holes. The laths are quite slim and the timber may split if you don't follow both steps.

Repeat stages 1 to 3 to make a second 'ladder'.

4 For this next stage you will find it useful to have a helper providing a second pair of hands.

Stand the two ladders upright with the points touching and the feet parallel and apart, creating a

square of 50cm (20in). You may find it useful to draw a square this size on the ground with line marker or chalk, to act as a base guide so that the bottom of your obelisk is exactly square. Using the position of the existing laths as a guide, attach more laths to the sides horizontally, cutting the ends flush with the existing laths.

5 The piece of 12.5cm (5in) square timber fixes on top of your obelisk and provides the base for the

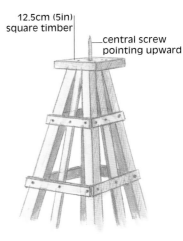

12.5cm (5in) square timber

central screw pointing upward

✿ Planting Variations

This obelisk will more than stand up by itself as a sculptural feature without the aid of any planting, but I am not averse to adding a climber or two if it is situated in a border that merits the addition of some vertical planting. The climber should not swamp it, nor should the strong outline be lost in a mass of complicated tendrils and stems, such as clematis. A climbing rose that is not too vigorous can be kept in check easily, the blooms are undeniably superb, and there are so many shades to complement the colour of your obelisk. I would suggest roses such as 'Constance Spry', 'New Dawn' or 'Zéphirine Drouhin'.

Above *Rosa* 'New Dawn'.

finial. Drill a pilot hole through its centre and screw the 7cm (2¾in) screw through the hole so that it protrudes 4.5cm (1¾in) on the other side.

Attach the square of timber where the uprights meet, using the 5cm (2in) screws, *with the central screw pointing upwards*. You will need to drill pilot holes to prevent the screws from splitting the timber.

6   Drill a pilot hole 5cm (2in) deep in the centre of your finial, if it doesn't already have one, and fix it onto the protruding screw on top of the obelisk.

7   Paint the obelisk with undercoat and then at least two coats of topcoat in the colour you have chosen. Be sure to get the brush into all the nooks and crannies as the paint will help to protect the obelisk against the elements as well as be visually pleasing.

KNOT GARDEN

If you want a garden feature that will look as perfect in winter as it does in summer, then you can do no better than a knot garden. This design combines box (*Buxus sempervirens*) and cotton lavender (*Santolina chamaecyparissus*) in a geometric pattern with the rows of plants seeming to weave in and out of one another. The contrast of the small, dark green, glossy leaves of the box against the fine silver-grey of the santolina is the key to the design's success.

There are thousands of designs for knot gardens. You can try to design your own but unless you want a contemporary design I would suggest you research some of the historic designs. You will find that almost every conceivable geometric pattern has been tried. I'm all for originality but there is no point in trying to re-invent the wheel.

The knot garden was a feature developed to be viewed from above, so there is little sense in siting it away from the house. Traditionally, the most formal, contrived features in a garden were sited next to the house, with the design becoming more natural as it blended into the surrounding countryside. Not many of us have a plot large enough to use this style of design to its full, but the principle remains the same. The best way to find a good site for your knot garden is to take a plan of the garden and draw lines at right angles from every window and doorway. Preferably, one of these lines should run through the centre of the knot. Never put the knot garden at an angle to your property. The site will need to be flat. A very slight slope would be acceptable but the design won't 'read' properly if there are undulations in the ground.

An intricate knot will need regular clipping to maintain the sharpness to the pattern, but I usually find the task more therapeutic than tedious.

Shopping list

Multi-purpose compost
Slow-release fertilizer granules
76 *Buxus sempervirens* plants, preferably in 3- or 5-litre (1.5 or 2.5lb) pots
20 *Santolina chamaecyparissus*
Geotextile membrane (optional), 4 x 4m (13 x 13ft)
Pea gravel to cover an area 4 x 4m (13 x 13ft) to a depth of 5cm (2in)

Tools & equipment

Spade
Trowel
Surveyor's tape
2 garden canes
Line marker paint

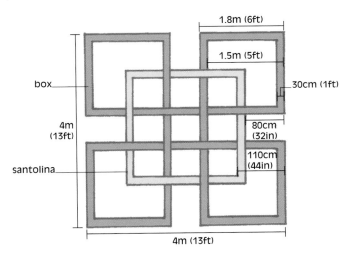

box

4m (13ft)

santolina

1.8m (6ft)

1.5m (5ft)

30cm (1ft)

80cm (32in)

110cm (44in)

4m (13ft)

1 Clear the site of all weeds and grass. Remove any hard landscaping, rake the site flat and remove any large stones.

2 Mark out the outer square of the design, 4 x 4m (13 x 13ft), on the ground in marker paint. Use the 3, 4, 5 triangle method (see page 132) to make sure that each corner is an exact right angle. The design won't work if this shape is not precise, so take your time and get it right. Make sure that the centre of the design is aligned with the view from your door, window or other viewpoint you have planned.

3 Mark a second square 30cm (12in) in from the first. Then another 80cm (32in) in, and then a final one 110cm (44in) in, measuring each time from the original outermost square.

You should now have four concentric squares. Use a string pulled taut or a wooden board to mark out these lines, as they must be absolutely straight.

4 Now mark 1.5m (5ft) and 1.8m (6ft) in from each corner of the outer square. Join each of these points with its partner on the opposing side, again using the straight edge.

It might look like a mess of lines but you now have the outline for the knot design.

5 To help make things clearer, colour in the channels for the box with some line paint. Keep referring to the plan as you do this and be especially careful to get the points at which the box weaves with the santolina right. The inner weave of box with box won't be clear until the knot has been clipped.

6 At last the planting! The box plants should be spaced with their centres about 30cm (1ft) apart, but you may have to shuffle the plants around slightly to fit the pattern. There must always be a plant at each corner point, but there is room for manoeuvre in between. Make sure that the plants run exactly down the centre of each channel and stand back frequently during planting to check your line is straight.

If the ground you are planting in was previously an area of hard

Right The patterns
you can use for a
knot garden are
limited only by your
imagination. In this
design, gravel in
three contrasting
colours helps to
define the pattern.

landscape and is very compacted, make the planting hole three times, not just twice, as big as the pot. Add plenty of compost and a handful of fertilizer granules to the earth and don't plant too deeply – there is a layer of gravel yet to be added on the surface.

7 Now add the lines of santolina plants, planted in the same way as the box plants.

❖ Planting Variations

A knot made without box loses some of its crispness; there is not another plant that can be clipped so small and tightly. But there are many alternatives to santolina. Lavender creates a lovely loose hedge with its soft grey foliage and spikes of hazy blooms, and some of the larger thymes have an incredible scent, with delicate flowers in shades from white to deep pink.

An evergreen knot will take about three years to shape up fully, but if you want instant impact you might like to try to create a woven pattern with annuals. Choose low-growing, solid plants such as *Salvia farinacea* 'Victoria', *Senecio cineraria* 'Silver Dust', californian poppies (*Eschscholzia californica*) or, for a slightly quirky feature, ornamental cabbage (*Brassica oleracea*), in shades of green with white to deep purple veins, which will certainly be a talking point.

❖ Project Links

As the knot garden is a very formal type of feature, a screen separating it from more informal areas of the garden would give it added impact and define its setting. In a large garden a hedge would be ideal, but in a small garden a less solid barrier such as the decorative screen on page 65 would be just right.

Two 2m (6½ft) screens would be the same length as one side of the knot garden, but it would look wrong to put the screen right up to the edge of the knot. Instead, leave a path around the outside of the design and use three screens on each side to be enclosed, omitting a central screen on one side for access.

8 The laying of geotextile membrane is a personal choice, and you may decide to spread the gravel straight onto the earth and around the plants. That will do very well, except that without the membrane the knot garden does become high in maintenance as you will have more work to keep the area weed-free and looking its best. If you decide to use a membrane, lay it in strips between the rows of plants, letting it run right up to the stems. Make small notches in it to allow you to push the fabric around either side of the plants' stems.

9 Finally, spread a layer of gravel over the entire area, to a depth of at least 5cm (2in).

Maintenance

The box will need clipping two or three times during the summer growing season and the santolina twice, once in spring and again in late summer after flowering. Never clip the knot by eye, especially the box. Use two canes pushed into the ground with a string pulled tight between them as a guideline. Check the height of the string all the way along and clip exactly to the line. The santolina has a slightly more 'woolly' outline and can be left a

little more untidy, but still use the string to keep the height constant.

Box will grow to up to 2m (6ft) tall if left unclipped but can be kept small and compact by regular pruning. I would recommend about 30cm (12in) wide and 40cm (16in) tall for this knot design. The santolina will find its own height, and when it flowers it will be larger than the clipped box; but you can be quite enthusiastic when clipping it back, as it has a tendency to become woody and tatty-looking if left to its own devices.

Tip

I have recommended gravel as a surface around this knot garden as it is particularly traditional for this type of feature. The simplicity of the knot lines is best viewed without the distractions of elaborate paving. Gravel will blend into the background and can also be spread right up to and under each plant, acting as a mulch, keeping the weeds down, the moisture level up and the look of the design neat.

HERB STEPS

Steps are traditionally constructed entirely from hard materials and are planned purely as a way of getting from one level to another. A generously proportioned herb step, or two, is a practical yet unusual feature that will attract attention and release a wonderful scent as you pass by. The design works equally well as a small retaining wall and can double as a scented seat.

One of the attractive features of these herb steps is their size. Steps are commonly made far too narrow. Make them at least as wide as the path they connect to, and whenever possible much wider. The steps in this project are 2m (over 6ft) wide, and, although only the middle section is meant for walking on, aesthetically they are wide and welcoming.

If your garden is on more than one level, you will probably know straightaway where you would like to site the steps. In a completely flat garden it is still worth considering adding a level change just to introduce another dimension into the design. Even one step up or down onto a terrace will create interest. Disposing of the soil you excavate to create the steps can be expensive and tiresome, so think about how to incorporate it into another part of the garden.

Feel free to change the dimensions of the steps, but remember to make every step the same size to make the flight easy to use. If your first step has a rise in level of, say, 20cm (8in), so should every other step in the flight. The same rule applies to the tread. If you allow these measurements to be

Shopping list

For one step:
Sand
2 railway sleepers, approximately
    20 x 10cm x 2m long (8 x 4in x
    6½ft), or oak or pressure-
    treated softwood cut to the
    right size
2 square oak pegs 20cm (8in)
    long x 2cm (¾in) wide
Topsoil, about 0.3cu m or 11–12cu ft
Herbs:
    Camomile (*Chamaemelum
        nobile* 'Treneague')
    Sage (*Salvia officinalis*)
    Thyme (*Thymus Serpyllum*
        'Minimus')
    Chives (*Allium schoenoprasum*)
    Creeping pennyroyal (*Mentha
        pulegium*)
    Parsley (*Petroselinum crispum*)

Tools & equipment

Spade
Wheelbarrow
Spirit level
Tape measure
Soft pencil
Right-angle rule
Wood saw
Silicone spray
Cordless drill with 2cm
    (¾in) drill bit
Mallet

random, the steps will be hard to climb and you are likely to fall. I would think that three steps would be the maximum amount you should build together. A level change any larger than that and you need to think about retaining walls and more substantial footings.

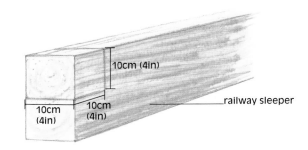

10cm (4in)
10cm (4in)
10cm (4in)
railway sleeper

1   Clear the area for the step, removing all grass and weeds, leaving an area 2 x 1m (6½ x 3ft) of flat earth. If you are working on a slope you will have to cut into it, and use the spirit level to ensure the base is level.

2   Spread a 1cm (½in) layer of sand on the base.

3   The first sleeper or length of timber is the front of your step. At each end measure in 10cm (4in), and, using the right-angle rule, draw a line round all four sides of the timber. On each of the 20cm (8in) sides, mark 10cm (4in) along the line you have just drawn. Again using the right-angle rule, draw a line up to the end of the timber on either side and join them across the end of the timber.

4   What you have marked up are two 10 x 10cm (4 x 4in) cubes, and you now need to remove one of these, as in the illustration above. Saw carefully, checking regularly to ensure that you are keeping to the guide lines on both sides of the wood. You may find when sawing such a big section of wood that your saw sticks, so the silicone spray should help to make the blade move more freely.
    Repeat steps 3 and 4 at the other end of the timber. Ensure that the cube you remove is on the same side!

5   Saw the second piece of timber in half to make two 1m (3ft) lengths. These will form the sides of the step. Cut notches from one end of each piece using the same method as before – steps 3 and 4.

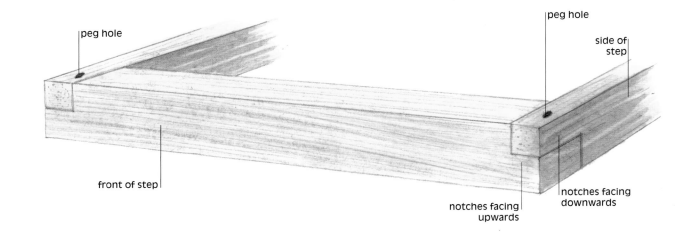

peg hole
peg hole
side of step
front of step
notches facing upwards
notches facing downwards

✿ Planting Variations

Herb steps will take general wear but not heavy wear. If you love the idea but need a harder-wearing step, add a central band of bark chippings where the heaviest footfall occurs, then plant the herbs on either side and they will grow around and into the bark. An unscented alternative is grass, giving the feature a green swathe that will stand up to tough use.

❖ Project Links

While the timber sleepers will take no end of wear, the camomile filling will not be suitable if the steps are used dozens of times each day or by lots of heavy-footed children. Instead of planting you could create a decorative mosaic for the tread.

The void that would have been filled with compost for the camomile will now need to be filled with a hard base. Hoggin is the best material you can use. Fill the area to just under 2cm (¾in) below the finished level of the step. Make sure that the hoggin is compacted well and then follow the mosaic instructions from step 2 on page 101.

10 Lay out your plants, putting the camomile down the centre of the step, with the thyme next to it, and finally the more delicate herbs on the outskirts where you will brush gently past but not trample them. Firm them in gently and water.

Left Allow the herbs to grow loosely and to self-seed around the area. Don't worry if you tread on them, they will take some footfall.

6 Place the front of the step on the ground with the notches facing upwards and the two sides at right angles to it with the notches downwards so that the ends interlock. Make sure the timbers are at right angles to each other. Mark 5cm (2in) in from the end and both sides and drill a hole all the way through both the timbers.

7 Now put the front of the step in place and the two arms at right angles. If you need to, adjust the amount of sand underneath to ensure everything is level – check with the spirit level.

8 Knock one oak peg into each hole using the mallet. It should fit tightly in the hole.

9 Fill the centre of the step with topsoil until it is flush with the timber. Tread down the earth to compact it and remove any air pockets. You need to do this firmly in the centre of the step where the foot traffic will go, and not so firmly at the sides. Top up the level of earth if necessary.

Tip

The one area unsuitable for timber steps is one of medium to heavy shade. Apart from the fact that the herbs would not grow well in the shade, the wood will develop a film of algae which can be slippery. This is easy to remove from stone steps with a pressure washer but on timber the washer will lift the grain.

herb steps **89**

SUN CANOPY

I always imagine myself treating my canopy on the lawn like a Bedouin tent, as I lounge on a rug with a pile of huge cushions. It's the perfect place to read the Sunday papers, enjoy an alfresco lunch or set the tone for a summer party. This is a real opportunity to experiment, as there are endless ways of adapting the design to fit in with the colour theme and look of your garden.

Canvas is available in colours from cool, elegant cream through to kitsch deckchair stripes. You may also consider adding fringes or draped fabric sides to turn it into more of a summerhouse. There are variations of material to be had, too. Rip-stop nylon, usually used for kites, is a great fabric and available in the most bold and brash colours.

The natural setting for a canopy like this is on grass, but if you don't have a lawn you could bed the tent hooks into paving. If the tension on the canopy is tight, then the legs should stand without being bedded in turf. Should you be fortunate enough to have a wall in your garden, you can dispense with two of the canopy's legs and attach the rope to two vine eyes that have been securely fastened to the wall.

This is a project that may well be hijacked by your children. They will love the idea of a 'den' in the garden, so be prepared to make two – one full-size one for you and one with half-size posts for them.

Tip

The canvas and bamboo are harder-wearing than you might imagine. Once erected, the canopy can stay outside during the summer and will be unaffected by gentle rain, but I would recommend that you dry and pack it away during the winter.

Shopping list

4 thick bamboo poles, 2m (6–6½ft) long and at least 5cm (2in) in diameter

12m (40ft) of rope, 5mm (¼in) in diameter

2.3m (7½ft) canvas 140cm (56in) wide. (You will find that fabrics come in standard widths. If the one you purchase is slightly wider or narrower, don't alter it, just use it as it comes.)

Eyelet punch and 4 10mm (½in) steel eyelets

4 hook-ended metal tent pegs

Tools & equipment

Power drill with 10mm (½in) drill bit

Sharp craft knife

Masking tape

Sewing machine

Cotton thread to match the canvas

Surveyor's tape

Line marker paint

Mallet

Trowel

1 Using the electric drill and 10mm (½in) drill bit, make a hole through one end of each bamboo pole, 5cm (2in) in from the end.

2 Cut the rope into four equal lengths, each one approximately 3m (10ft) long. Temporarily bind each end of the rope with masking tape so that it doesn't fray.

3 Follow the splicing technique illustrated on page 92–93 to make a loop at one end of each length of rope. This looped end is for anchoring the canopy to the ground with the tent peg.

4 Hem the cut edges of the canvas or fabric. Fold over about 1cm (½in) and then fold it over on itself again to conceal the cut edge. Press in place and sew. (If you are using nylon rather than canvas, iron through a cotton cloth or the heat will melt the fabric.) You could sew by hand but it would be much harder work. It won't be necessary to hem the long sides as they will have selvedged edges.

Below Using white canvas gives the canopy a chic, modern look which is just right for this contemporary design.

5 Mark a point in each corner of the canopy 4cm (1½in) from both edges and insert one eyelet in each corner with the eyelet maker.

6 Take one length of rope and one pole. Thread the end of the rope without the loop through the hole in the pole, then through one of the eyelets. Splice this end into a loop, as shown right.

Repeat for each of the other three corners.

7 Using the line marker paint and surveyor's tape, mark a rectangle, 1.6 x 2.4m (5½ x 8ft), on the area of lawn where you want to site your canopy. Don't worry about the lines; it is only the corner marks that are important.

8 It is almost impossible to put up the canopy alone. You will need at least one helper and if possible three would be ideal.

With one person on each corner, put the bottom of each bamboo pole on a marked corner point. Then, putting tension on the rope, pull the loop to the ground and when the canopy is taut with no creases you can knock the tent peg into the ground and hook the rope loop over it.

The structure works best if the poles are leaning slightly. If you find the legs slip on the ground, you can make a small divot with a trowel and wedge the pole into it.

Splicing a rope

This may seem a lot of trouble for little reward when you can easily tie the rope with a knot. However, the trick with features such as these is attention to detail. A perfectly spliced loop will last a very long time and look professional.

Terms you will need to know:
Lay manufacturer's twist on a rope

Unlay to unwind or take apart a rope

Standing part remaining rope you have not unlayed

Unlay a short piece of the end of the rope. About 8–10cm (3–4in) will be enough but experience is the best teacher and you may find you like more; it is better to unlay too much than too little. Stop the unlaying moving any further by tying a thread around it.

Loop the rope around to form an eye and arrange the three strands as illustration 1.

Start with the central strand and tuck it under one strand of the standing part against the lay (see illustration 2).

Take the
strand that is
towards the inside of the
loop and tuck it under the
next strand round of the
standing part, at the same
level (see illustration 3).

Now turn the whole thing over
and tuck the remaining strand
under the remaining standing
strand – this is the only one left at
the same level which does not have
a strand under it (see illustration 4).

Make another round of tucks in the
same lay: take a strand over its
adjacent standing strand and tuck it
under the next standing strand.
Do the same with the two
remaining strands. The
action is over, under,
over, under.

3

Make three full tucks, and
then cut off the excess
strands close to the
standing part to create a
neat finish.

4

❖ **Project Links**
The canopy is initially intended as a shade for a
lawn, to escape the sunshine, but it can be used
to create the most stunning party venue. If you
place four canopies on four sides of a central
square you will create a dance floor surrounded
by canopied areas for dining and seating. With the
addition of a further piece of fabric at the back of
each canopy, the courtyard becomes enclosed.

Lighting will complete the party atmosphere
(see page 76). Spotlights can be placed behind the
canopies and shone either at the back fabric, so it
makes a coloured screen of light, or from the
base of each pole up into the canopy roof. Candle
lanterns can be hung in rows along the guide
ropes, secured in place by some more wire.

2

Two Weekend Projects

Above The construction of this project
could be adapted to a three-sided canopy
like the one on this terrace.

CHILDREN'S PLAY FORT

It is very rare to find a garden where children live which does not have at least one bright-coloured play toy. They are great fun, but plastic in primary colours doesn't do much for most garden schemes. This wooden play fort is suitable for children from two years upwards, and you will be amazed how long it remains popular, even for teenagers as somewhere to 'hang out'. So even though it requires a lot of work and some expense you will get plenty of use from it.

The natural wood will allow the fort to blend with its garden surroundings. If you would like to colour the fort to fit into your garden scheme, use one of the water-based stains that are readily available in an ever-increasing colour range. Children will climb all over the fort, so a stain will survive and weather better than an exterior paint. You could further soften the outline of the fort with climbing plants; opt for sturdy-stemmed plants that are more likely to survive the hordes of children.

Take some time thinking about the best place to position the fort. There is always a compromise to be made between having active play areas like this close to the house for reassurance and far enough away that the ensuing noise and chaos doesn't disturb the rest of the household – but at least the fort's attractiveness need not also blight the view! Choose an area close enough to keep an eye on them but far enough away to give both you and them some privacy. Wherever the fort is placed make sure that there is easy access to it – don't expect children to use narrow paths that wind through your garden design; they will always take the direct route from the door to the fort, even if it runs through a flower border.

A flat piece of lawn is a good site for the fort, but mowing up to the uprights is a nuisance. Add a border of bark chippings around the outside with a straight edge of lawn to cut up to.

Dimensions for the fort are based on the diameter of the 10cm (4in) poles, so measurements here are more precise than for some projects. Stick either to metric or imperial, especially for the cutting guide, as the measurements given are equivalents, not exact conversions.

1   Begin by marking an equilateral triangle on the ground. First choose where you want the front face of the fort and mark a line 2.5m (8ft 4in) long with the line. Use a piece of string between two garden canes or a wooden board to ensure that the line is exactly straight. Put a cane through the end of your measuring tape and spear it in the ground at one end of your line. Pull the string taut, measure 2.5m (8ft 4in) and scribe an arc. Repeat this process at the other end of your line, and the point at which the two arcs cross is the third point of the triangle. Mark straight lines to complete the ground plan of the triangle.

2   Mark the central point of each line, 1.25m (4ft 2in) in from each

corner. Use the string and canes to make a straight line connecting each of these central marks with its opposite corner point. Where the lines cross is the centre of the triangle, the position for your tree.

3   Cut the timber into lengths using the cutting list on page 96.

It is worth laying the lengths on the ground next to the space they will occupy. If you leave them in a pile for sorting later, it gets very confusing. Each post will need thorough sanding at the sawn end that will be above ground, to get rid of sharp edges and splinters.

Shopping list

66 tanalized round fence posts
    10cm (4in) diameter x 2m
    (6½ft) long
12 steel bolts, 20cm (8in) long x
    10mm (½in) diameter
10 x 80-litre (40lb) bags of bark
    chippings
1 tree
Geotextile membrane (optional)

Tools & equipment

Surveyor's tape
Line marker paint
Garden canes
String
Soft pencil
Wood saw
Rough sandpaper
Wide chisel
Mallet
Spirit level
Large lump hammer
Small timber offcut
Cordless drill with 10mm (½in)
    drill bit
Spade

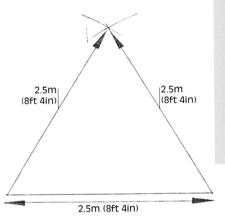

2.5m (8ft 4in)   2.5m (8ft 4in)

2.5m (8ft 4in)

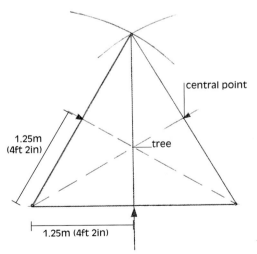

central point

1.25m (4ft 2in)   tree

1.25m (4ft 2in)

✿ Planting Variations

The central interest of this feature is a tree. You might choose to leave it out of your design but I think that would be a mistake; the tree softens the scheme as well as giving shade. There are so many alternative trees to choose from; the snake bark maple (*Acer pensylvanicum*) or the paper bark birch (*Betula papyrifera*) are interesting choices for a small tree, as is lilac (*Syringa vulgaris*) if grown with a single stem. If you have the room, you may opt for a more traditional large tree such as oak (*Quercus robur*) or horse chestnut (*Aesculus hippocastanum*).

An area of garden, such as the fort, that is all their own is a good opportunity to introduce children to the idea of growing their own plants. Try some climbing beans on the sunny wall of the fort. They are easy to germinate and fast-growing, as are sunflowers (*Helianthus annuus*). They will grow in almost any soil and the really tall varieties will appreciate the corner posts which can act as supports.

Above *Acer pensylvanicum.*

Components cutting list

Uprights:		metric	imperial
6	x	1.9m	74in
6	x	1.8m	70in
6	x	1.7m	66in
6	x	1.6m	62in
6	x	1.5m	58in
6	x	1.4m	54in
6	x	1.3m	50in
6	x	1.2m	46in
6	x	1.1m	42in
6	x	1m	38in
6	x	90cm	34in
3	x	80cm	30in

Horizontal poles:			
3	x	1.9m	74in

This will leave you six poles uncut: three are crossing poles and three are corner uprights.

All the upright poles, including the full-length corner poles, will need to have a point at one end. Do this with the chisel and mallet and make sure that the point is even or you will not be able to drive the post in vertically.

4 Begin by hammering in one of the corner posts, using the timber offcut to cushion the hammer blows so you do not damage the post top. Check with the spirit level that the post is exactly upright. Stop when 1.6m (62in) is above ground level.

5 Hammer in the rest of the posts so that the posts drop and then rise in level by 10cm (4in) per post. Check regularly that the posts are upright and following the line.

6 Place the first crossing pole between uprights number 6 on opposite sides of the triangle. Drill a pilot hole through the crossing

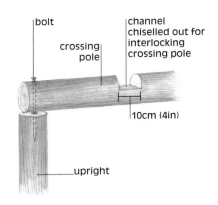

pole vertically into the upright, and screw in a steel bolt. When you lay the next crossing pole in place you will need to mark with a pencil the point at which it touches the first pole. Using the mallet and chisel gouge out a channel from both pieces of wood so that they lock into one another.

Repeat until all three pieces are in place and bolted.

7 Place the three horizontal poles in position between uprights number 4. Drill a pilot hole through the horizontal pole into the upright and screw in the steel bolt.

8 At the centre point of the fort, which you marked earlier, dig a planting pit twice the size of the container that your tree comes in and plant it, firming the root ball well in. It is hard to say whether you should feed the tree up through the frame or drop it down; you will have to judge for yourselves which will damage the tree least, but usually roots are more important than foliage.

9 Clear the surface inside the fort of weeds and grass and cover with a 10cm (4in) layer of bark chippings. You may choose to add a geotextile membrane to suppress weed growth but you will find that it is easily scuffed up by small feet and can sometimes cause more problems than it solves.

ORIENTAL SCREEN

The simplicity, harmony and understatement of oriental-style gardens makes them very appealing, but they are often difficult to get right, and the whole ambience can be ruined by unsympathetic boundaries. The use of bamboo makes this an ideal screen for an oriental garden, although I would use it in any scheme that relies on natural materials. You may be making a small area within your garden into an oriental garden, in which case these panels would make a very suitable dividing screen that would blend well into the rest of the garden.

These screens have a tall, elegant proportion. The panels can be made any height or width you need, although don't make them too wide as bamboo has a tendency to bend if it is spanning too great a gap. The panels are inexpensive to construct and if you have a pile of broken or old garden canes then you have half the materials already.

If you want to use these panels as a boundary between you and your neighbour make sure that you own the boundary before you start ripping out the old one. Even if the boundary is yours, talk to your neighbour first to discuss your ideas, if only to preserve good relations. Should you find that the boundary is not yours and you cannot persuade your neighbour to let you replace the fence anyway, just put your new fence in front of their old one. You will have to sacrifice a little of your plot to do this but it will be worth it to get the right effect.

Shopping list

For one panel (multiply the amounts according to the length of fencing):

5 tanalized 10 x 2cm (4 x ¾in) timber lengths 2.4m (8ft) long

2 tanalized 5 x 2.5cm (2 x 1in) posts 2.4m (8ft) long

50 zinc-plated screws, 3cm (1¼in) long

2 bags of post mix

Lots of bamboo garden canes. For one panel you will need around 200 lengths 1m (3ft) long – broken longer canes are fine.

1 Mark out accurately where your fence is to go – don't rely on an existing fence line if you are removing old panels. Use a length of string between two garden canes or a long wooden board to ensure that all the panels will be in a straight line. Draw the line on the ground with line paint.

2 Make a mark on the line with line paint every 1.10m (3ft 2in).

3 At every mark on the line dig a hole 50cm (20in) deep and 30cm (12in) across.

4 On one of the 10cm (4in) wide pieces of timber draw two lines along its length 2.5cm (1in) in from either side. You should have two parallel lines 5cm (2in) apart. Do the same on a second piece of 10cm (4in) timber.

Tools & equipment

Surveyor's tape

Canes and string or long wooden board

Line marker paint

Spade

Soft pencil

Cordless drill with screwdriver fitting

Watering can or hosepipe

Wood saw

Spirit level

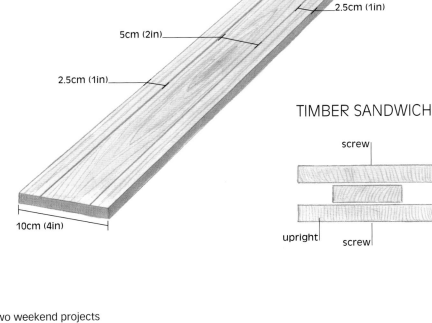

pencil line

2.5cm (1in)

5cm (2in)

2.5cm (1in)

10cm (4in)

TIMBER SANDWICH

screw

upright   screw

5 Each upright is made up of two wider timber lengths sandwiching a narrower length, creating side slots that will hold the bamboo canes. Use the pencil lines to position the 5cm (2in) 'sandwich filling' exactly and screw the larger pieces of wood to the smaller. You will find that the timber is quite soft and the screws will counter-sink themselves. One screw every 20–30cm (8–12in) will be fine.

Repeat steps 4 and 5 to make as many uprights as you need for your fence.

6 Make a pencil mark on each post 50cm (20in) from the bottom.

Tip

You can, if you like, make an aperture in the screen to enable you to see through to another part of the garden. When you are sliding the canes into place, put short canes the size you want your 'window' vertically in the slots either side, and then continue to stack the canes above them in the same way as before.

Left Be inventive with bamboo. It's a very easy material to use: simply attach one piece to another with copper wire and bind the tie with raffia or soft stems.

Place one post in each of the pre-dug holes with the slots sideways, facing each other. Check that their pencil lines are all at ground level, so that exactly the same amount of post shows above ground.

7   Put the post mix around the base of the posts and check that they are all vertical in both planes. While the post mix sets you might find it useful to attach a temporary length of timber to the posts to act as a brace.

8   Saw the bamboo canes into 1m (3ft) lengths. If you are incorporating 'windows' in the panel (see Tip) you will need fewer than the 200+ canes needed for a solid screen.

9   Once the posts are firm, slide the canes in between the two slots, building them up until they reach the top of the posts.

10 Attach the extra flat timber to the top of the fence panel with a screw through the top of the post.

Left Bamboo or reed fencing can be used to good effect when only partial privacy is needed. Spacing the canes allows light to filter gently through.

MOSAIC

I absolutely love mosaics. They give you chance to express your artistic ability and, more importantly, to add a motif that makes your garden your own. Multi-coloured tiles in bold, brash designs may be exciting in a Mediterranean setting but, unless this is the theme for your garden, such bright patterning may look out of place. Instead, this uses pebbles in subtle shades from muted blues, pinks and creams to dark greys and blacks, to create a mosaic that looks good in all weathers and settings.

I have suggested a pebble and slate design but your imagination can run riot and it would be much better if you took inspiration from my design and created your own. There are myriad materials available to use for mosaics. Be imaginative. I have used broken slates, set on edge rather than flat, to add texture to the design. You will also find that if you are using offcuts you may get them for free. Pebbles are available in bags, either sorted into colours or in mixed bags for sorting yourself – a great job for children to help with.

It would be wonderful to create a whole terrace in which a pebble mosaic wove in and out of the slabs. However, it is much more likely that you have an existing terrace that you would like to make a little more individual. Lift a section of slabs in the middle of your terrace to make a central feature, or a single slab at the beginning of a pathway to give a welcoming start. If you are attempting an edging mosaic, lift the last but one row rather than the last row, as the mosaic is more stable if it is contained within a border of slabs. One word of warning: the pebbles do not provide a perfectly flat surface so they may not be suitable for the elderly or very young.

This is a great project for spring. The cement mix is easy to use but it will not set properly if the conditions are very wet or if the temperature is likely to drop below freezing.

Shopping list

Small pebbles, in shades of
    white, grey, black and blue
Broken blue slate
Cement
Sand
*(1 small bag of cement should be
enough for a mosaic the size of
one or two paving slabs, and you
will need five times the amount
of sand.)*

Tools

Newspaper or brown paper
Marker pen
Wheelbarrow
Gardening gloves
Spade
Bucket of water
Line marker paint
Trowel
Long spirit level
Stiff brush

1 Once you have decided which design to use and where you want to site it, remove the existing slabs or bricks and dispose of them. Scrape out the ground below the slabs to a depth of about 5cm (2in) from the slab surface.

before you mix the cement. Draw your design on paper with a marker pen – freehand will be fine. Then arrange the pebbles in the pattern, moving them around so you get the right combination of colours and shapes.

2 Grade the pebbles into piles of shape, size and colour to help when building up your pattern. You may like to have a dry run

3 Mix up the cement and sand in a proportion of 1 cement to 5 sand. I find a wheelbarrow is the best vessel to use. Always wear gloves

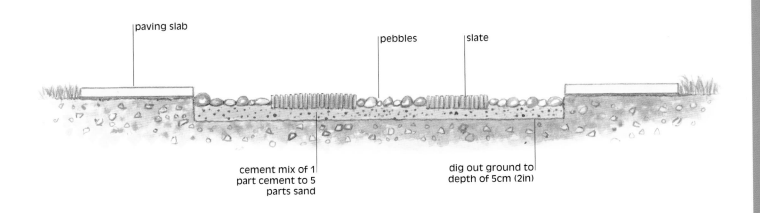

paving slab

pebbles   slate

cement mix of 1 part cement to 5 parts sand

dig out ground to depth of 5cm (2in)

mosaic, especially if you have extra helpers. When transferring the pebbles and slate, put the basic outline in first and then put the fill-in pebbles around it.

Press the pebbles firmly into the cement. They should be at least half, if not three-quarters, buried in the mix. The lower they sit the flatter your finished mosaic will be. The difficulty is that the finished level of cement must be the same as the surrounding paving, otherwise the mosaic will become a pond when it rains. But as each pebble is pushed in it displaces some cement, so raising the level. It is really a matter of balance, but I find it is easier to take excess cement out than to try to add some later.

5   Every few pebbles, use the straight edge of the spirit level to check that they are all approximately the same height. Don't feel you have to complete the mosaic at breakneck speed. The cement will take at least four hours to set, although the weather might have an effect on the setting time.

Above Bright colours aren't essential to create a contrast. This swirling pattern shows how effective just two shades of pebbles can be.

as the lime in the cement is corrosive and can irritate your skin. If you get it on your face wash it off immediately. Mix the cement well to the consistency of smooth cream cheese. If it is too wet the pebbles will sink, but if it is too dry you won't be able to press the pebbles in far enough. Test a pebble in the top of your barrow load of cement.

4   You now have two options. You can either fill the entire mosaic area with the cement mix and transfer your pebbles directly from their pattern on the paper guide, or you can mark out the design using the line marker and then put the cement into the area in sections. As scary as it sounds, I favour the first option unless you have a very large, ambitious

TURF SCULPTURE

Something as simple and utilitarian as a lawn can become a unique feature if you turn part of it into a turf sculpture. The elegant undulations in the turf give you places to nestle, sitting out of sight of the household mêlée or blasting wind. Children will turn small mounds of earth into imaginative play houses, castles and mazes. Have you forgotten the sheer exhilaration of rolling down a grass slope?

Shopping list

Amounts will depend on the shape and size of your sculpture. When you have drawn your design to scale, calculate the ground area it covers, make a note of the height and take these measurements and drawing along to your supplier, who will be able to work out how much you will need.

Topsoil
Turf or grass seed (see opposite
    for tips on choosing)

Tools & equipment

Line marker paint
Stepladder (if you need a
    vantage point from which to
    see your design)
Garden canes and string for
    scribing curves
Spade
Wheelbarrow
Scaffold planks or long wooden
    boards

Below Carefully sculpted turf features create the perfect centre piece for a seating area.

The design of your sculpture will work best if it follows organic, flowing lines. There are a few illustrations here to start your imagination going, but the sculpture will be more individual if you make up your own design. Look to nature for inspiration, in the shapes of leaves, flowers and stones. Allow space for gentle inclines – mowing steep slopes will be awkward, and a petrol mower will cut out if it is tilted beyond a certain angle.

Realistically you will need a minimum of about 3sq m or 30sq ft to create a mound that will have impact, but the larger the area the better. An area of existing lawn will be most suitable to start with but there is no reason why you cannot start from scratch with an area of uncultivated land or border. Ensure that the area is free of perennial weeds before you start. Although grass is a resilient plant, very heavy shade is not the best place for a turf sculpture, neither is ground that is waterlogged. A dry area is fine if you can keep it watered.

This is a great project for the autumn or spring, although avoid any hard wear on your lawn if there has been a lot of rain; you will compact the ground and exacerbate any water-puddling problems.

I can't deny that it will take more time and skill to mow undulations than a flat surface, but once you get into a routine the time needed to care for the mounds is far less than any flower border. A hover mower will cope best with the banks. I would suggest you keep the blades on a high setting so that the grass is not cut too short; this will give the sculpture a more lush look, as the mounds will have a tendency to dry out on the high points.

SOME DESIGN SUGGESTIONS

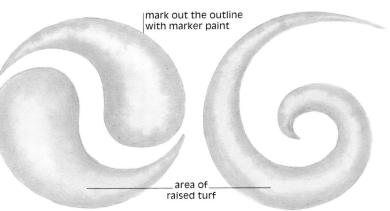

mark out the outline with marker paint

area of raised turf

1 Draw out your sculpture outline on the lawn with line marker paint. Take your time and get the shape right – if in doubt make it larger rather than smaller. Look at it from a high vantage point. An upstairs window would be best, but otherwise climb up a stepladder for a better view. The sides of the mounds should be gentle slopes not vertical cliff faces (remember, you have to mow them!), so allow room for them to taper.

Curves can be drawn freehand, but if the design is looking too 'woolly' you could use a cane and string and scribe any curves as part of a circle.

2 Start to move the topsoil into the shape of the design. If you are working on an existing lawn lay a path of scaffold planks over your route so that your wheelbarrow and feet don't cause too much damage to your remaining lawn.

3 When you have about 20cm (8in) depth of soil, tread it down with your boots using a small shuffling motion. You will look like a penguin but this is the most effective way to compact the earth to get rid of any air pockets. If you don't do this the mounds will look fine at first but as the soil settles dents will appear in your once smoothly rounded shapes.

4 Keep adding soil, shaping and compressing until the mound is the shape and height that you require. This is an art, not a science – keep stepping back to look at the

Above This natural armchair looks as though it has just risen out of the meadow around it.

mound from all angles and make sure that the edges taper gently into the existing lawn.

5 After a final 'penguin walk', gently rake over the mound to loosen the surface of the soil, and remove any stones completely.

6 You can now cover the mound in two ways, either by seed or turf (see box). Seed is less expensive but requires more patience.

❖ Seed or turf?

Seed

As the area is likely to get heavy wear, choose a seed mixture containing rye grass, a hard-wearing type. Distribute over the mound according to the supplier's instructions and rake the surface lightly to incorporate the seed. You will need to keep a close eye on the seed to make sure that it doesn't dry out. The seeds will germinate and emerge in about 7–14 days. Allow the grass to reach 5cm (2in) tall before mowing.

Turf

The quality of turf you buy is a personal choice. 'Fine lawn' is rich emerald green with no weeds and each strand of grass is narrow and delicate. However, if the sculpture is to take any wear then I would go with ordinary 'meadow turf', which is hard-wearing and much less expensive.

Lay the turves in the same pattern as a brick wall and make sure that each turf butts up tightly to the one next to it (see page 49). On a flat lawn you would usually use a long plank to press them down. Obviously you can't do this with undulations so you will need to press down with the flat of your hand, especially over the joins. Stay off the lawn until the sods are knitted together and keep the area watered if the weather is dry.

❖ Project Links

The turf sculpture has a contemporary look about it when it is sited as the centrepiece of an area of lawn. It can look stark. Surrounding the sculpture with a wildflower meadow (see page 54) would give it a soft and natural landscape setting. The way you blend the two will depend on the design you have chosen. As a general rule I would use mown turf on the high mounds of the design and let the surrounding meadow flowers run into the design where it meets the sculpture. For easy access and to enhance the design, add a mown path to the sculpture through the meadow. You don't necessarily have to take the most direct route – meander, or create a chicane.

As some of the process for these two projects is the same, I wouldn't be surprised if the combined work only took two weekends.

These projects are mini-gardens in their own right if you only have a tiny plot, but if you are fortunate enough to have room then creating all six will keep you busy for many weekends!

THREE WEEKEND PROJECTS

3

Three Weekend Projects

POTAGER

A potager is simply an ornamental kitchen garden. Combining an area of productive vegetable and herb beds with decorative paths, trees and flowers is a lovely alternative to 'the vegetable patch', and this design is small enough to fit into most domestic gardens or as part of an overall design in a larger garden. The potager's planting is dependent entirely on your personal culinary taste – should you wish, there is no reason why you cannot devote the whole site to soft fruit or salad crops.

Left Pack your herbs tightly into the pattern to create formal lines. You will be cropping from them all summer which should keep them small and neat.

Three Weekend Projects

Shopping list

10 tanalized 5 x 5cm (2 x 2in) timber lengths, 2m (6½ft) long
40m (130ft) tanalized edging board, 20 x 2cm (8 x ¾in)
200 zinc-plated screws, 4cm (1½in) long
8 screw-in vine eyes
1 roll of heavy-duty garden wire
1 tonne of good topsoil
10 x 80-litre (40lb) bags mushroom compost or well-rotted manure
4 standard bay trees (*Laurus nobilis*), about 1.5m (5ft) tall
1 wooden obelisk, about 2m (6ft) tall (see page 80)
4 cordon apples in different varieties
Geotextile membrane, about 8sq m (85sq ft)
6 x 80-litre (40lb) bags bark chippings
selection of vegetable and herb seeds or plants

Tools & equipment

Garden spade
Wheelbarrow
Surveyor's tape
Line marker paint
Wood saw
Wood chisel
Mallet
Electric drill with a screwdriver fitting and small drill bit
Spirit level
Border fork
Wire clippers
Scissors
Secateurs
Soft garden string

For this project, more than any other in the book, you need to think very carefully about its site. First, it needs to be flat. You can get away with a slight slope if it only goes only one way, but you will find that a formal pattern like this looks best on a flat plane. It is beautiful enough to merit a site close to the house, where the symmetry and restrained order can be appreciated from an upstairs vantage point. A formal feature like this should be in line with paths or vistas that run at right angles from the house. Think about allowing an existing path to run through the potager, using the material of your existing path rather than using bark for the paths of the potager.

This potager is intended to be used as the small productive area of a larger garden. However, if you only have a very small plot, then think about adapting the design. The essence of this project is its symmetry, so any adaptations that you might make will need to retain this order. Removing the inner square bed completely, leaving just the four surrounding beds, would give you a central area for a table and chairs for outside dining. A firmer ground surface, such as paving, would then be better than loose bark chippings, which are likely to leave you with a permanently wonky table.

Vegetables and herbs will need to have good light levels. You will not have much success if you site it in the shade, but a compromise of dappled or partial sun will do nicely. A potager of this size won't give self-sufficiency for a family, but there will be enough room to grow all the herbs, salad and some small vegetables. It will also be an introduction into the art of productive gardening that you may be tempted to expand into other areas of your garden.

1 Clear the site. If it covers an area of existing lawn, strip the turf but don't dig over the ground. Remove all hard landscape materials and plants.

2 Using a scale plan, mark out the design on the ground using the line paint. First measure out the outside square. Each side should be 4.6m (15ft) and the square

Crops for your potager

Here are a few planting ideas, but this is only a guide – your choice of what to grow in your potager will be up to you and your tastes.

For a long period of cropping and to avoid a glut, make successive sowings from early spring right through the summer of:

Radishes

Spring onions

Spinach

Carrots

Beetroot. The leaves will bring a rich purple to the potager's design.

Lettuce. Choose a variety of different types – some are very decorative.

Leeks. These are slow to mature, so will be a constant presence in the potager throughout the growing season. Sow at the end of winter for autumn and winter harvesting.

Runner beans for the obelisk. Delay sowing until late spring; they don't like late frosts but grow fast.

Herbs might include chives (*Allium schoenoprasum*), sage (*Salvia officinalis*), parsley (*Petroselinum crispum*) and thyme (*Thymus vulgaris*). Sage comes in several different leaf colours, all edible, and there are many different varieties of thyme.

When growing vegetables, whether in a potager or an allotment, it is wise to operate a crop rotation system. This is not as complicated as it may sound – it simply means growing each crop in different beds each year. The object is to deter the build-up of soil-borne pests that might damage your crop, and to allow the soil to maintain a balance of nutrients.

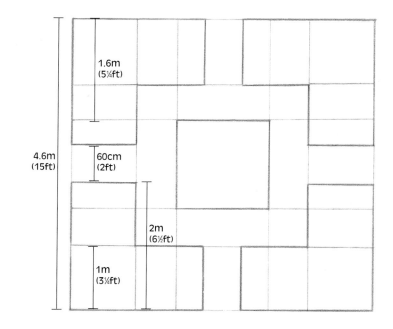

must have right-angled corners; don't let it become a parallelogram. When you have finished marking out the square a good check is to measure the diagonals; if they are the same then you are spot on.

3 Next, mark 1m (3¼ft) and 2m (6½ft) along each side from the corner points. Join these with their opposing mark on the other side of the square to make a grid pattern. You should now be able to mark out the L-shaped vegetable beds from these guidelines. Next, measure 1.6m (5¼ft) along each side from the corner points and connect each mark to its opposite one. This will give you the inner square and leave 60cm (2ft) paths.

4 Cut eight of the tanalized timber lengths into four, to give you 32 stakes each about 50cm (20in) long. Chisel one end of each stake into a point. Do this as symmetrically as possible, because if the point is lopsided you will find it more difficult to knock it into the ground without it twisting.

5 Using the wooden mallet, knock one stake into the ground at each corner point of the L-shaped beds and extra ones halfway along the outer sides. Leave 20cm (8in) of stake above the ground – the amount protruding should be over rather than under; you can saw the excess off later. Put the stakes on the inside of the marked line, apart from the inner corner stakes which must be placed on the outside of the lines.

6 Attach the edging boards to the stakes using the screws and electric drill. You will need to stagger the position of the screws so that they don't run into each other. Use the spirit level to ensure that the boards are all level, otherwise when you get to the last board you'll find that it doesn't match the first one. Make sure that the bottom of the board is flush with the earth, any gap will cause problems when you fill the beds.

7 From the remaining two timber lengths cut four 60cm (2ft) lengths and make a point at one end as described in step 4.

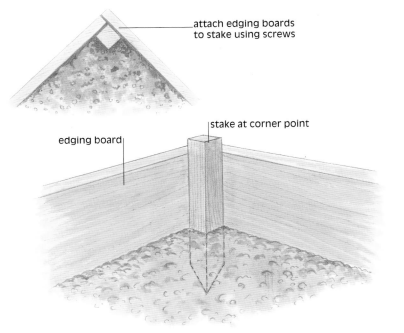

attach edging boards
to stake using screws

edging board

stake at corner point

8 Knock one stake into each corner of the central square, leaving 30cm (1ft) above ground. Drill a pilot hole for the vine eyes 2cm (¾in) down from the top of each stake and screw in the vine eyes.

9 Attach the wire to each side of the square, threading it between pairs of vine eyes. Pull it taut and wind the end of the wire neatly around the vine eye.

10 You can now loosen the earth at the bottom of the L-shaped vegetable beds. It is not necessary to dig over the ground; just release the compacted soil. A fork will probably be the easiest tool to use. Fill the beds with the topsoil to about 5cm (2in) below the top of the boards.

11 Add two bags of compost per bed and fork in gently. Don't stand on the earth. The beds are narrow enough for you to stretch to work on the beds without compacting the soil.

12 Plant the bay trees, one in each outside corner of the L-shaped

beds. Make sure that they are planted at the same depth as they were in the pot.

13 Gently fork over the central bed and add the remaining two bags of compost. Position the obelisk in the centre of this bed.

14 Plant one fruit tree at the centre of each side of the inner square. Now make a cut through the main stem to a height of about 30cm (1ft). Having just paid for a perfectly good tree, to cut it in half may seem incredibly brutal but you will find that the tree will now grow out from either side of the cut, producing horizontal branches. As these branches grow, tie them into the horizontal wire with soft string.

15 Cut the geotextile membrane to the size of your paths and lay it down. Hold it in place with rocks while you empty the bark chippings on top. Spread the chippings out evenly and remove the rocks.

❀ Planting Variations

Your potager's crops will be entirely according to your taste, but you could also ring the changes with the structural planting. The four bay trees have a culinary use but they are mostly there to give definition to the end of the beds and continue the theme of formality. Standard forms of box (*Buxus sempervirens*) or holly (*Ilex aquifolium*) should be easy-to-find alternatives. Instead of the step-over apples you could use a herb to define the central square. Chives will give a low informal line of foliage during the summer along with delicate lavender flowerheads, or a low hedge of thyme would provide shape for both summer and winter. You will need to keep it well trimmed to stop the plants becoming unruly and you may have to sacrifice some of the flowering season in order to do this.

❖ Project Links

The obelisk project (see page 80) is an ideal centrepiece for your potager.

If your garden is tiny, not much larger than the dimensions of the potager, you could adjust the design to give you room for a seat from which to enjoy the garden. The oak bench (see page 60) would suit the potager admirably.

To keep the design true to its original plan but incorporate the bench, remove adjacent arms on two of the L-shaped beds (you will need to make this alteration at step 3, when you are marking out). This will leave you with two rectangular beds and a gap 2.6m (8½ft) wide between them – plenty of space for the bench and the necessary leg room in front.

Setting the bench directly onto the bark chippings or earth floor would be unstable. You will either have to put paving under the entire area or two slabs directly underneath the bench's legs. These can be covered with a fine layer of bark once the bench is in place, if you wish to maintain the natural look of the garden.

PERGOLA

If I had to plan a garden using only one design feature, a pergola would be my choice, especially on a new plot. New gardens can take years to mature, and a pergola will quickly give the impression of maturity and give much-needed height while the planting catches up. This design is fairly traditional but uses rope rather than timber for the overhead beams. This means that there is no complicated joinery to tackle and so it is well within everyone's capabilities to build.

Shopping list

20 tanalized 10 x 10cm (4 x 4in) timber uprights, 3m (10ft) tall
20 bags of post mix
50m (170ft) hemp rope, 3cm (1¼in) in diameter
Galvanized C-shaped nails (about 600)
Roll of garden wire
Soft string
5 x 80-litre (40lb) bags of good-quality compost
20 summer jasmine (*Jasminum officinale*)
18 white lavender bushes (*Lavandula* 'Alba')
Chipped bark or gravel to cover approximately 30sq m (300sq ft)

Tools & equipment

Garden cane
Surveyor's tape
Line marker paint
Spade
Electric drill with 3cm (1¼in) drill bit
Mixing board
Spirit level
Large bucket or dustbin
Gaffer tape
Stepladder

A pergola's primary purpose is to provide a structure for plants to scramble over and it might seem a wasted opportunity to use only one type – with 20 posts you could have 20 different plants. This is quite true, but the pergola could look overdressed and messy with climbers of many different sizes, shapes and colours, and in this case I think that the use of one type of climber will give continuity and elegance to the design. If you would prefer to use several different climbers, then keep the continuity by choosing ones that all have the same coloured blooms.

Unlike most pergolas that run in a straight line or with the occasional angled turn, this is designed as a sweeping curve. This makes it perfect for gardens that have an awkwardly shaped corner, or a triangular plot with a pointed end. In a long thin plot don't assume that the pergola must go at the far end. This will look good and will be an enticement to visit the end of the garden, but you could also site it so that it obscures the view of the rest of the garden and creates an attractive screen that makes you want to explore the hidden area beyond.

The walkway could have any type of material underfoot, but I have used bark as it is easy to lay and blends well with the central grass circle. Gravel is another good option, and you could also gravel or pave the inner circle.

1 Mark out two concentric circles on the ground, using the line marker paint. Put a cane at the centre point of your circle and, using the surveyor's tape pulled taut, draw a circle of 3m (10ft) radius and one of 5m (16ft) radius. Leave the cane in place.

2 Decide where you would like the entrance to your pergola and mark on the inner circle where the first inner post will be. With the tape pulled taut, measure along the line of the inner circle 1.5m (5ft) from the position of the first post and mark the position of the second inner post. Continue round the line of the inner circle until you have marked ten inner posts. Check that the entrance and exit of the walkway are where you want them to be. If not, rub out the post marks and start again.

3 When you are happy with the orientation, mark the outer posts. Do this by hooking the beginning of the tape onto the cane in the centre of the circles and pulling it taut so that the tape passes exactly over the first inner post mark. Where the tape passes the outer

circle, make a mark. Repeat until you have ten outer post marks to match the ten inner ones.

4 Dig a hole 30cm (1ft) across and 50cm (20in) deep at each post mark.

5 At one end of each length of timber upright mark a point 10cm (4in) from the end and in the middle of the post. Drill a hole through each upright with the 3cm (1¼in) drill bit. At the other end of the post, mark a pencil ring 50cm (20in) up: this is where ground level will be when the post is in position.

6 Put one post in each hole with the drilled hole at the top pointing towards the centre of the circle.

7 Mix up a bag of post mix and concrete each post into its hole, making sure that the pencil 'plimsoll line' is exactly at ground

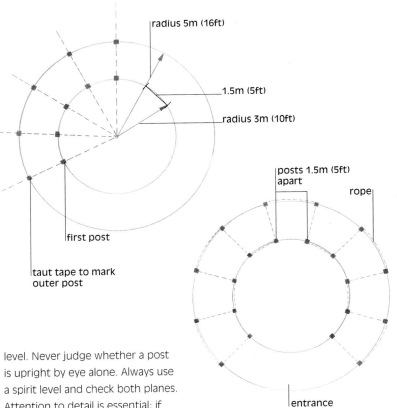

radius 5m (16ft)

1.5m (5ft)

radius 3m (10ft)

first post

taut tape to mark outer post

posts 1.5m (5ft) apart

rope

entrance

level. Never judge whether a post is upright by eye alone. Always use a spirit level and check both planes. Attention to detail is essential; if one post is not exactly upright the whole pergola will look wrong. Make sure that the concrete finishes a little below the ground level so that you can cover it with earth to disguise the block.

8 Soak the rope in water for at least an hour before threading it through the posts. This will give you a better line and make the rope soft and easy to handle. If you don't have a bucket large enough to soak the rope in, use a dustbin. Tie a knot at one end of the rope then thread it through the holes in the pattern shown. You might find it useful to wrap some gaffer tape around the 'needle' end of the rope to make it easier to pass through the holes.

9 On the three sides of the timber uprights not facing inwards knock in a 'C' nail every 20cm (8in); then take the garden wire in a line from top to bottom through each nail.

Fasten the ends of the wire tightly. This may seem time-consuming but the jasmine is not able to attach itself to the wood and will need the wire to twine its stems around in order to climb.

10 Dig a planting hole on the outer side of each of the inner posts. You will have to allow for the concrete base, and the hole should be twice the size of your jasmine containers. Plant a jasmine at the base of each post, using a mixture of the soil you have dug out and new compost. Tie in the stems to the wire using soft string, and water even if it has been raining.
    Repeat the process on the outer line of posts.

11 Plant the lavender, two plants in each space between the outside posts, following the original circular line.

❀ Planting Variations

Both jasmine and lavender appreciate a good dose of sunshine, so you will need to bear this in mind when you are choosing the site for your pergola. If your pergola is to be in dappled shade then consider changing to a rose such as *Rosa* 'Constance Spry' or 'Madame Alfred Carrière'. Both have soft pink blooms and will easily cover the upright posts without swamping the structure. Of the two, 'Constance Spry' has the better scent and slightly stronger-coloured blooms. As a shade-happy alternative to the lavender, I would add a low hedge of *Alchemilla mollis* (lady's mantle).

   All these suggestions come into their own throughout the summer but if you wish to add some interest for the rest of the season plant random drifts of naturalized crocuses: *Colchicum autumnale* for autumn and *Crocus vernus* for spring colour.

SLEEPER PATH

A path should be a feature in its own right, but it can often end up as the poor relation in the garden. Time and money will be lavished on terraces, lawns and borders and then the paths to connect them are thrown down with little thought, using whatever materials are left over. This is different, a subtle combination of hard and soft materials that is both practical and beautiful, and easily adapted to your colour scheme or personal plant preferences.

Each square in the design after the first adds 90cm (3ft) to the length of the path. You will need 2 sleepers for each design repeat and 1 extra to make up the shortfall in the outer edges at the end of the run.

Railway sleepers or treated
    timber, approximately 20 x
    10cm (8 x 4in) and 2m
    (6½ft) long
Geotextile membrane
Sand
Fine crushed gravel
Turf
Fritillaria, either as bulbs in
    autumn or, in the green,
    in spring
Muscari, either as bulbs in
    autumn or, in the green,
    in spring

Tools & equipment

String
Garden canes
Line marker paint
Scaffold board
Spade
Wood saw
Silicone spray
Large right-angle rule
Large spirit level
Sharp knife

Right *Fritillaria meleagris.*

The timber framework and the simple planting of this design blend harmoniously together to form a mini border, lawn and path all rolled into one. It will fit into many different settings and is a good way to join landscape materials together, to introduce a material from one area to a material from another by constructing a path out of both.

Your path will need a reason to exist. There is little point in putting all the effort into it if there is nowhere for it to go. It could be used to connect one terrace with another or join a doorway to a seating area. If you will see your path as it runs at right angles to your property, then be sure that you line up the path exactly with a window or door. This will give a feeling of harmony and the opportunity to site something to catch the eye, perhaps a sculpture or another feature, at the end of the view.

This project would not be suitable for a layout that required a curved or snaking path. It is intended for a straight line, but you can quite easily make right-angled turns. In fact, it would make a great feature if you built it on all four sides of a square lawn, to form a boundary between grass and border.

1 Lay out the area for the path using string tied to a couple of garden canes. Make two parallel lines 1.4m (4⅔ft) apart. Make sure that they are parallel all the way along and that this path outline corresponds to any windows or doors that you are trying to create a vista from. When you are satisfied, mark the lines with line marker paint.

2 Excavate the area to a depth of 12cm (5in). Use the scaffold board laid along the line to help you to cut an accurate straight line.

3 Cut the railway sleepers into lengths of 60cm (2ft). If you have 2m (6½ft) sleepers then you will get two 60cm (2ft) lengths plus one 80cm (2½ft) length out of each one. The shorter lengths are for the inner squares and the longer ones for the outside edge. You can cut timber of this thickness with a hand saw; it is quite hard work, but the silicone spray will help stop the saw sticking. If you feel confident, you could use a chainsaw, which will make light work but won't be as accurate. Go slowly and carefully and be sure to use all the safety equipment provided.

4 Line the bottom of the trench with a sheet of geotextile membrane so that it covers the earth and turns up at the sides of the trench. Add a layer of sand about 2–3cm (1in) thick in the bottom of the trench, then lay the long sleepers end to end, broad side up, along either side of the trench. Use the spirit level to check that they are level, adjusting the sand underneath if necessary. You don't need to worry about drainage or adding a fall to this path as water will drain away freely through the planted areas.

5 Put a cane in the ground at one end of the path 10cm (4in) in from the inner edge of your sleeper. Match it with another at the other end of the path. Tie a string between them and mark a straight line with the line paint. Repeat on the other side. These new guide lines, which should be 80cm (2½ft) apart, mark the outer edges of the central squares. Don't be tempted to miss out this stage and try to place the sleeper squares by eye. The pattern is a geometric one and will look awful if it is not exactly square.

6 Lay the shorter lengths of sleepers in the square pattern shown, with

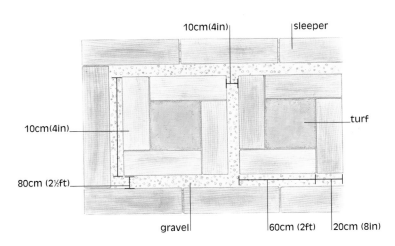

10cm(4in)   sleeper

10cm(4in)

turf

80cm (2½ft)

gravel   60cm (2ft)   20cm (8in)

the lines as a guide to make sure that the sides stay true. Use the right-angle rule to make your corners square. Check that the square sleepers are level with the edging ones using the spirit level, and use more sand if necessary to raise the sleepers to the correct height.

7 Fill the areas between the sleepers with the topsoil from your excavation. As you return it, remove any large stones, weeds or grass. Gently tread the earth to compact it. Do this more firmly in the central squares where the grass is going to be than in the trenches for the bulbs. Fill the trenches to 2cm (¾in) below the top of the sleepers.

    If your soil is very heavy or wet, then mix some of the gravel into the soil for the bulb trenches before you return it. This will help it become more free-draining, which is a better growing condition for the bulbs.

8 Turf over the central squares, cutting the grass to shape with a sharp knife. You shouldn't have to join any sods together as each square is quite small; but, if you do, ensure the edges are butted up tightly together. Press down the turf with a length of timber so

that it is level with the sleeper and then water it well. It is best not to walk on the turf for a week or two until it starts to knit together and take root into the earth.

9 Scatter the bulbs into the trenches in a random fashion and plant them at a depth of twice their own height. If you would rather have an instant effect then buy your bulbs 'in the green', which means in pots as fully grown plants, usually sold in flower. You will find that they are about four times as expensive this way, but it is easier to get an instant effect than by planting as dry bulbs. Whichever way you choose, plant several of the same type together, not dotted in one among another.

10 Fill the trench with gravel until it reaches the same level as the sleepers. Press it down firmly. This is less fiddly to do if you have planted dry bulbs instead of plants.

Maintenance

The lawn section in the centre of the path can be mown over very easily as it is flush with the timber. The only time you will have to take care is when the bulbs are in the green. Then, as there is only a small amount of lawn, you can use a pair of garden shears for clipping the grass.

❀ Planting Variations

The side channels are suitable for almost any small bulb planting. Try miniature daffodils such as *Narcissus* 'Tête-à-tête', or the little blue *Scilla siberica*. For a bolder colour scheme, cyclamen are fantastic in-your-face flowers. If your path is in an area of dappled to heavy shade a drift of lily-of-the-valley (*Convallaria majalis*) will look exquisite.

    The central squares of turf are an integral part of the design, but if you really can't face clipping then use *Soleirolia soleirolii* (mind-your-own-business). Remember, however, that even though it isn't grass it will need some clipping to keep the regular shape.

Above *Narcissus* 'Tête-à-tête'.

MINIMALIST GARDEN

The art of minimalism, whether in gardening, interiors or any other form of artistry, is an exercise in restraint. A garden that is big, blowsy and full of plants and features will absorb your mistakes, but a minimalist scheme leaves no room to hide. This project is one of the hardest in the book. It involves dry walling, pouring concrete and quite complicated laying out, but the reward is obvious: you will have created a self-contained haven of stillness.

You do have to be a certain type of person to love this look. You may naturally be very neat and regimented, but if, like me, you are a chaotic person, this project can make a wonderful antithesis to the rest of your less ordered garden. It uses all the mantras of design, such as echoing shape and the use of a single material or single colour, and sticks to them as if they were law.

It is quite probable that you have a section of your garden, tucked down the side of the house or in an awkward corner, that would be perfect for this feature. Don't be put off because the design is square. You will need to create a square in order to draw the oval correctly, but it is quite easy to extend the final perimeter afterwards to reach into an odd shape.

Concrete is an ancient material, perfected by the Romans. It has been used ever since with varying degrees of success. Unfortunately, during the 1960s concrete was used to construct hideous tower blocks and its beauty was lost, but now it is enjoying something of a revival. This garden uses concrete in two forms, as a liquid poured into a mould to take on the curves of the design and as pre-cast slabs. Inexpensive and unattractive in their original state, they are broken to reveal hidden depths, then stacked in a bold, modern shape.

Don't be tempted to add more planting to the scheme. By all means make changes, but stick to one or two varieties. Remember, restraint.

1 Using the line marker paint, mark out a square outline for your minimalist garden. Each side should be 4m (13ft) long. Be very exact in your right angles (see measuring a 3, 4, 5 triangle, page 132) and when you think you have the measurements right check the diagonals: they should be exactly the same.

2 With the string and canes, make a diagonal straight line between two opposing corners and mark it on

measuring a 3, 4, 5 triangle, page 132

bench   bamboo

alchemilla and   concrete ball on   concrete path
eremurus   gravel and planting

Shopping list

12mm (½in) plywood sheet, 2.4 x 1.25m (8 x 4ft)
Rough-sawn timber for stakes, about 30, each 30cm (1ft) long
Hardcore (amount as for concrete)
Ready-mixed concrete, approximately 2cu m (3cu yd), but take your measurements along to the supplier, who will calculate
Concrete slabs, broken – the equivalent of 100 60 x 60cm (2 x 2ft) slabs
Large galvanized dustbin
7sq m (75sq ft) of turf
Soleirolia soleirolii (mind-your-own-business)
1 small bag of white gravel
1 concrete ball, 30cm (1ft) in diameter
6 x 80-litre (40lb) bags of multi-purpose compost
Phyllostachys aurea (bamboo)
Alchemilla mollis (lady's mantle)
Eremurus (foxtail lily)

Tools & equipment

Line marker paint
Surveyor's tape
String
2 garden canes
Wood saw
Spade
Wheelbarrow
Lump hammer
Gloves
Goggles
Jig saw

the ground with line marker paint. Also mark 1.5m (5ft) along the sides from these opposing corners.

3   Place two canes firmly in the ground 1.5m (5ft) in from each corner point along the diagonal line. Tie the string in a loop so that it is taut between the two canes and reaches one of the 1.5m (5ft) marks you made on the sides.

Below Almost any type of slab or natural stone can be stacked to form a seat. Here blue slate is softened by planting in the cracks.

4   If you keep the string taut at all times and walk slowly around the two canes, drawing a line with the line marker paint, you will scribe a perfect oval which will touch the outer square at the four points you have marked.

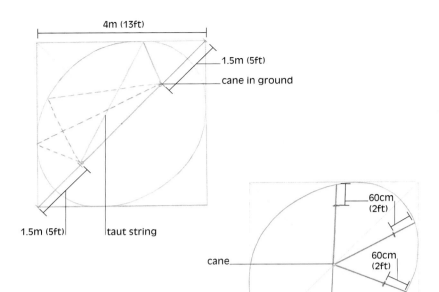

5   Now put a cane in the ground at the centre point of the square, where the two diagonals cross. Loop the end of the surveyor's tape over it and then pull it taut. Repeatedly measure 60cm (2ft) in from the oval, marking with the line marker paint again, until you have a second oval marked inside the first.

6   Cut the plywood into strips 20cm (8in) wide.

7   Using the plan, mark two lines to indicate the beginning and end of the concrete seat. The rest of the area between the two ovals will become the path. Excavate this to a depth of 15cm (6in).

8   Use the plywood strips to make a mould, following the curve of the path and held in place with wooden stakes. Then fill the area with hardcore, compacting it well to form a base 7–8cm (3in) thick. You can then pour in your ready-mixed concrete and tamp it down in order to get a smooth surface with no air bubbles.

9   Once the concrete has set, you can begin to build the seating area. The concrete slabs will need to be broken up into smaller sections. Use the lump hammer and don't forget to wear gloves, as well as goggles to protect yourself from flying concrete chips.

As you break the slabs sort the pieces into piles of small, medium and large chunks. This will make it easier when you are assembling the seat.

The art of building the seat is the same technique as dry-stone walling. Each piece must be arranged so that the broken face is facing outwards. The seat is not held together with cement, only

large piece of concrete to make seat

mix of small, medium and large chunks, broken face outwards

Left *Eremurus* (foxtail lily).

Below *Alchemilla mollis* (lady's mantle).

❀ Planting Variations

The planting in a minimalist scheme needs to be simple and refined. This design would lose its elegance if the borders were crowded with a mixture of plants, so keep the choice to one or two. The background screen of bamboo stems could be exchanged for a wall of yew (*Taxus baccata*). This can be clipped into a solid shape to fill the triangle and could then be 'fenestrated' by the addition of a window cut in the shape of an oval to further echo the dominating motif. The other triangular border would look stunning as a single block of *Heuchera* 'Palace Purple', the deep red leaves offset against the white concrete.

Where the original planting scheme was yellow and orange, this alternative is deeper, so to complement the very dark green yew and purple/green heuchera, choose a dark purple bulb such as *Tulipa* 'Queen of Night' or *Fritillaria pyrenaica*.

If you were dead set against mowing you might replace the central turf with a camomile lawn (*Chamaemelum nobile* 'Treneague' is the best), or dispense with green altogether in favour of white gravel or crushed glass.

❖ Project Link

It is an extremely easy mistake to add too many features to a design like this. Restraint is a very difficult skill to master and this is not a project that needs extra adornment. Having said that, the small water feature on page 62 would fit extremely well into this minimalist scheme.

The little pool could simply replace the galvanized circle of *Soleirolia soleirolii* and white gravel, or it could be further adapted to echo the ovals of the overall design. You could place the water tank in the centre of the layout and then expand the slate edging to occupy the whole of the inner oval.

As both these projects have fiddly details and should not be rushed, allow more than four weekends to complete the combined work.

carefully arranged pieces. Use the larger ones on the outside graduating to the smaller ones. Don't go to the next level until the first one is completed and all the pieces are stable. If they rock, remove them and start again.

Reserve some of the larger pieces and finish the top layer with these, to make a flat seat.

10 With the jig saw, cut a section from the top of the dustbin about 10cm (4in) deep. Position it within the central area, off-centre so that one side just touches the concrete path and the top rim is flush with the path.

11 Prepare the ground for turfing (see page 49). Turf the inner oval area, cutting round the galvanized dustbin circle.

12 Create a small earth mound in the central part of the dustbin circle and plant up with the *Soleirolia*

soleirolii. Fill the area between the mound and the dustbin ring with white gravel and then place the ball in the mound of planting.

13 Fill the triangular area behind the seat with the bamboo, and plant the alchemilla and eremurus in the other triangular area outside the oval. Water them in well.

PEBBLE STREAM

Flowing water in a garden always fascinates. It can play many roles – masking background noise, encouraging wildlife, adding an element of movement – but most of all it has the same hypnotic attraction as the flames of an open fire. This stylized stream has been designed to suit both traditional and contemporary settings, and, although it takes some skill to construct, the result is definitely worth all the work. The copper will discolour with age to a wonderful verdigris effect and the cobbles will show different shades when wet or dry.

The mixture of copper with cobbles is an unusual one, and makes this a feature that looks as good in an urban plot as in a country garden. But think carefully about how to site and orientate your stream – the copper wall will need sympathetic surroundings. A wall or solid boundary would be an ideal backdrop. You could, if you wished, dispense with the stakes that anchor it and instead mount it directly onto the wall (leaving enough room between for the water pipe from the pump). A gravel path that ended at the foot of the stream would be particularly effective: the gravel would merge naturally with the cobbles of the stream bed and the copper 'well-head' would provide a focal point at the end of the view along the path. The cypress trees complete the framing of the picture and will lead the eye naturally to the copper. *Cupressus sempervirens* is the slimmest of the cypresses and remains pencil-thin even when mature.

Feel free to play with the length of the stream. It is possible to shorten it if you have little room and, equally, to extend it. Having the stream run the entire length of an existing path would look wonderful, although it may need a larger pump. Take advice on the right size of pump from the supplier, and make arrangements for a qualified electrician to install the electricity supply; this is not a DIY job.

Shopping list

- 25mm (1in) exterior grade plywood board, 33cm x 1m (13in x 39in)
- 15mm (½in) copper sheet, 38cm x 1.5m (15in x 5ft)
- 10 copper tacks
- 2 tanalized 5 x 5cm (2 x 2in) timber stakes, 1m (3ft) long
- 6 zinc-plated screws
- Plastic header tank (water tank) approximately 60cm (2ft) diameter and 60cm (2ft) deep, square or round
- 3m (10ft) plastic water pipe
- 1 bag of post mix
- Sand (three times the amount of cement, see below, plus allowance for lining the stream bed)
- Butyl pond liner, 2.5 x 1m (8 x 3ft)
- Cement (about 2 small bags, depending on the length of your stream and the size of your pebbles)
- Pebbles
- Water pump
- 2 jubilee clips
- 30cm (1ft) copper pipe, 1cm (¾in) diameter
- Clear mastic sealant
- 3 steel reinforcing bars, approximately 80cm (2½ft) long
- Steel wire mesh, approximately 80cm (2½ft) square
- Geotextile membrane, 1 x 1m (3 x 3ft)
- Extra-large 'dinosaur-egg' cobbles
- gravel
- 6 *Cupressus sempervirens*

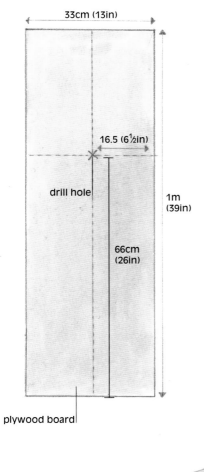

plywood board

33cm (13in)

16.5 (6½in)

drill hole

1m (39in)

66cm (26in)

board

copper

Tools & equipment

Soft pencil
Surveyor's tape
Drill with 15mm (½in) drill bit
Hammer
Nail
Line marker paint
Spade
Spirit level
Plasterer's trowel
Craft knife
Gloves

1 Measure halfway across the plywood board and make a pencil mark 66cm (26in) up from the bottom. Drill a hole through the board using the 15mm (½in) drill bit. This is the hole for the water pipe.

2 Place the copper sheet over the board, making sure that it is exactly central. Gently hammer the copper

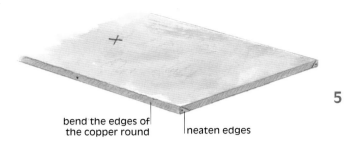

bend the edges of the copper round | neaten edges

so that the sides bend around the board. Turn it over, so the copper is beneath the board, and work your way around the board, bending the copper's edges round and neatening the corners like folded bed sheets.

3 When you are happy with the corners, attach the copper to the back of the board with the copper tacks, three on the long sides and two on each short side.

4 Punch a hole, using a nail and hammer, through the centre of the pipe hole in the wood. Turn the board face up and make a cross shape in the copper so that you can bend the sides neatly through the hole in the board.

5 Attach the stakes to the back of the board about 5cm (2in) in from each side, and with 'legs' sticking out of the bottom edge by about 50cm (20in). These are what will anchor the board into the ground at the head of the stream.

6 Using the surveyor's tape and line marker paint, mark out the channel for the stream. It should be 1.8m (6ft) long by 33cm (13in) wide. Place the plastic tank in position at the foot of the stream so that it overlaps slightly. Mark the outline on the ground.

7 Dig out a hole the same size as the tank and then a gently scooped trench for the stream. It should be approximately 20cm (8in) deep at its deepest point and graduate to ground level. Check with the spirit level that there is a slight fall from the head of the stream to the tank; a drop of 2cm (¾in) should be plenty. (Allow 1cm (½in) per metre/foot fall if you are making a longer or shorter stream.)

8 When the trench is finished, dig a small gully for the plastic water pipe along the bottom of the trench. Lay the pipe in it, ensuring that there is 80cm (2½ft) of pipe spare at the copper wall end.

9 Place the copper wall at the head of the stream and mark the position of the two legs. Dig a rectangular hole that is 50cm (20in) deep and a little wider than the legs.

Put the copper wall in position, making sure that the plastic water pipe is underneath and protrudes behind it. Fill the hole with post mix to just a fraction below ground level. Use a spirit level to check the

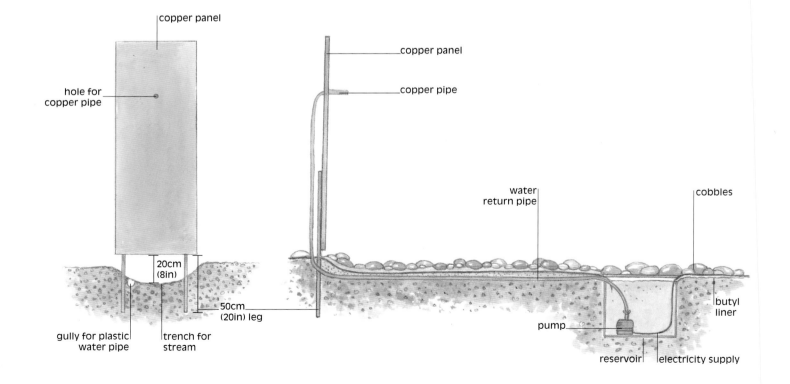

copper panel

hole for copper pipe

20cm (8in)

50cm (20in) leg

gully for plastic water pipe | trench for stream

copper panel

copper pipe

water return pipe

cobbles

butyl liner

pump

reservoir | electricity supply

wall is exactly vertical and prop it upright until the mix is firm.

10 Fill the trench for the stream with sand to a depth of 2–3cm (1in), covering the water pipe and sculpting the profile to a pleasing curve. Pat the sand firmly with your hands.

Lay the butyl liner over the sand, making sure that it butts up exactly to the copper wall and ends with an overhang in the water tank. Remember not to cut the excess butyl off.

11 Mix the concrete, 1 part cement to 3 parts sand. Spread this to an even thickness of 5cm (2in) in the bottom of the trench, extending out to the same width as the copper wall. The areas either side will be covered with cobbles, but these do not need to be cemented into place as the water does not run there.

12 Starting at the copper wall, begin to press the cobbles into the cement mix so that half of each cobble is showing and half is buried. The cobbles should run

across the stream in random lines so that the water will have to run around them, thereby creating greater movement.

If you don't want to tackle the whole stream at one sitting you can lay the cement and press in the cobbles in stages, working in, say, 50cm or 18in strips.

Be as neat as possible and wash the cobbles before you use them. Wipe them with a slightly damp cloth if you get cement on them. Make sure that the cement is set round the cobbles before you move on to the next step.

13 Get the electricity supply for the pump installed. Fill the water tank with water and connect the pump to the water pipe with the jubilee clip. Lower the pump into the water. You will find that your pump has a restrictor valve on it. Turn this so that the flow is very low. You can adjust it later if you decide you want more water.

14 Switch off the pump and connect the other end of the plastic pipe to the length of copper pipe using the other jubilee clip. Push the

Tip

A great advantage of this feature is that it can be made safe for a garden used by children. The only deep water is underneath the wire mesh in the tank, so if you want to make it doubly secure from inquisitive fingers, make a frame for the mesh with a hinged side that can then be padlocked into place. Even the most ingenious of children won't be able to get it open.

copper pipe through the hole in the copper wall so it protrudes at the front by about 25cm (10in).

Before you secure the pipe, test the water flow. Turn the pump on again and within a few seconds water should flow from the pipe. Decide how far you want the copper pipe to protrude and adjust the flow valve on the pump to get the volume of water right. Once you are happy with the flow, fix the copper pipe into place with the clear mastic sealant.

15 Lay the reinforcing bars, evenly spaced, across the top of the tank. Lay the sheet of metal mesh on top of them and then cover with the geotextile membrane. On top of the membrane arrange the dinosaur-egg cobbles and more pebbles to link it to the stream bed and dress the edges with gravel to hide the edges of both the mesh and the membrane.

16 Plant the trees, evenly spaced, on either side of the stream. Cut a cross in the butyl if it is in the way, and, when the trees are firmly planted and watered in, cover the ground surface around them with a layer of gravel.

Left The sound of moving water rushing over pebbles will add excitement and drama to your design.

PAVING MAZE

Mazes have been popular garden features since the eighteenth century, when they provided recreation, exercise and a secluded area where you could meet your lover for a clandestine kiss. The pattern of this maze is created by bricks set into a lawn: follow the right route and you will be rewarded with the perfect spot to relax under the shade of a special tree.

Traditional hedge mazes take many years to develop and involve a lot of precise clipping. This ground-level version gives you an immediate labyrinth to thread your way around, but is surrounded by a dense, rich green hedge of holly that will soon create a sense of seclusion, should you wish to indulge in a spot of clandestine kissing! However, you may have to share the feature with children who will love the puzzle of a maze.

To accommodate the maze as described below needs quite a large area of flat ground, nearly 7m (over 20ft) square, although you could reduce the size by leaving out the holly hedge. Of course, if you have more room you could expand the design and lay out a more complicated maze. Keep to the concentric squares at 60cm (2ft) intervals to maintain a balanced pattern.

A feature such as this will naturally draw attention to the tree at its centre, so choose a specimen that merits such star treatment. A particular favourite is the tulip tree (*Liriodendron tulipifera*), with its unique, flat-ended leaves and, in time, greeny-cream tulip-shaped flowers. The black mulberry (*Morus nigra*) is a much under-used tree that recalls a bygone era, which would make it an appropriate partner for the maze. It has beautifully gnarled bark and, after 15 years or so, delicious raspberry-like fruits. A flowering cherry, such as *Prunus* 'Shirotae', has spectacular double white blossom in spring, or consider the decorative *Betula papyrifera*, a birch that has paper-like peeling white bark and lively autumn colour.

Shopping list

Sharp sand
Terracotta bricks or paving
    blocks, sufficient to trace out
    58m (190ft) of maze path
    when laid end to end
42 whips of holly (*Ilex
    aquifolium*) for hedging
Compost and slow-release
    fertilizer
1 tree
Circular metal tree seat
1 metal archway approximately
    1m (3ft) wide and 2m
    (6–7ft) high

Tools & equipment

Surveyor's tape
Garden canes and string
Line marker paint
Half-moon cutter
Scaffold plank or wooden
    straight edge
Spade
Rubber mallet
Spirit level
Brick guillotine and goggles

hedge
60cm (2ft)
tree seat
60cm (2ft)
gap in hedge
6.6m (21ft)
tree canopy
brick
gap in hedge

1 With the surveyor's tape, canes and string, mark out the outer perimeter of the maze as a square 6.6m x 6.6m (21 x 21ft) with perfect right angles (see instructions for a 3, 4, 5 triangle, page 132). Check the diagonals are of equal length and then mark the perimeter and diagonals with line marker paint.

2 Mark out four more concentric squares inside the first, at spacings of 60cm (2ft). You will find the

Above An area used as a terrace or driveway can be crafted into a maze by the addition of some subtly placed setts.

Opposite To avoid the trouble of construction you can create a maze such as this by simply allowing your lawn to grow for a couple of weeks and then mow in the pattern.

Tip

There are so many variations on this theme that I hope this project can be the starting point for your own ideas, making the design original to you. You might like to fill the turf strips with small spring bulbs – snake's head fritillary (*Fritillaria meleagris*) would look especially charming – or even sow cornflowers and poppies for a bright summer look.

easiest way to do this is to mark off the corner points for these inner squares along the diagonals at 85cm (33in) intervals from each corner and then join them up.

3 Orientate the plan of the maze so that the single entrance is facing the correct way for your garden layout. The four inner squares form the maze. Following the plan, mark the pattern of the maze, scuffing out the marker line where there are gaps.

4 Dig out a trench one brick's width along every line (not the outer perimeter). Begin with a half-moon cutter to get clean, straight lines (you will find it helpful to use a long plank of wood as a straight

edge) and then excavate the trench 1cm (½in) deeper than your brick.

5 Scatter a 1cm (½in) layer of sand in the bottom of the trench, then, starting at one corner, fit the bricks into the pattern. Use the rubber mallet to bed the bricks firmly into their sand base. You can raise or lower their level by adding or removing sand. Check regularly with the spirit level that they are level, although it is more important that they sit flush with the lawn, so that you can mow over the top of the maze.

You will find that you need to cut bricks to make them fit. A brick guillotine is easy to use, although make sure that you are wearing goggles as you often get flying chips of brick.

6 When the maze is complete, dig a trench along the perimeter line about 30cm (1ft) wide and deep. Mix the compost and slow-release fertilizer into the excavated soil and plant the holly whips 60cm (2ft) apart, leaving a space 1m (3ft) wide for the entrance.

7 In the centre of the design you should still have a cross where the two diagonal lines meet. Plant the tree at that point and then position the tree seat around the trunk.

8 Fix the metal arch in position at the entrance to the maze. As the holly grows, clip it to form a neat shape around the arch.

Maintenance

The holly should be clipped once a year into a formal, straight-sided hedge. Keep the grass well mown and trim it back if it starts to encroach on the brick pattern.

✿ Planting Variations

Holly will give you a dense evergreen hedge in keeping with a traditional maze. A good alternative, if you would prefer a more relaxed, natural-looking hedge, would be a mixture of hawthorn (*Crataegus*) and blackthorn (*Prunus spinosa*). These will provide fantastic blossom in the spring and red berries in autumn, attracting a multitude of wildlife to feast and nest in them. To keep the same theme, the central tree could also be a hawthorn, which is allowed to grow into a loose standard.

If expense is not an issue then any of these thorns can be bought as bare-root saplings in the winter. Beech (*Fagus sylvatica*), only slightly more expensive in bare-root form, will provide a more formal hedge that, although deciduous, will keep its golden brown leaves throughout the winter, gales permitting.

Three Weekend Projects

It is possible to have a garden without hard landscaping, but it's not easy to access space without paths or terraces. However, just because a surface is useful, it doesn't have to be uninteresting. Once you are familiar with the practicalities of materials you can use your imagination to use them in original ways.

THE PRACTICALITIES
OF HARD LANDSCAPING

INTRODUCTION

Each project takes you through the stages of construction step by step, but there are certain general points that apply to a variety of different projects, whether in this book or not. You may also have decided to vary the groundcover surface from the one described in the project you are constructing, so this section will help you get the effect you want, with a professional finish. See the table in 'Hard Landscaping' (page 38–39) for the pros and cons of different materials and how best to use them.

3, 4, 5 triangle

You can mark out a perfect right angle using a surveyor's tape, three garden canes and a helper (you can do it alone, but it is trickier).

Insert cane 1 into the ground at the point that you require a right angle and attach the end of the tape to the cane. Measure 3m along the side of the square you are marking out and insert cane 2. Loop the tape around the cane and extend the tape to 12m. Tie the tape to cane 1 at this point. This will leave a loop of tape. Next, look back along the loop of tape to find the 8m point. Holding this point, gently pull the tape until it is taut between canes 1 and 2, and the point you're holding. When it is taut, insert cane 3, making sure that where you insert it corresponds exactly with the 8m mark and that the tape is still tight all around the triangle.

You have now created a triangle made up of sides measuring 3, 4 and 5m in length, and the angle at cane 1 is exactly 90 degrees; a perfect triangle.

> **Tip**
>
> If you are working with an imperial tape, use the yard markers in just the same way – it's the ratio of the numbers that is important, not the actual measurements.

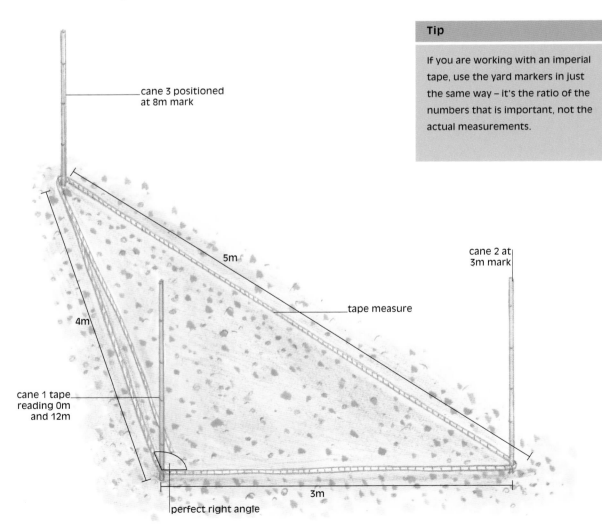

cane 3 positioned at 8m mark

5m

cane 2 at 3m mark

tape measure

4m

cane 1 tape reading 0m and 12m

perfect right angle

3m

GRAVEL

This is the easiest surface to lay, requiring only a sturdy base. It also goes down very quickly, if you are looking for a 'quick fix' surface. These instructions apply to an area of gravel used as a path or terrace. If you were to use the area for vehicle access you would need to increase the depth of the base material by a minimum of 50 per cent and use an industrial roller to ensure good compacting.

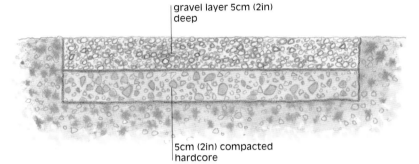

gravel layer 5cm (2in) deep

5cm (2in) compacted hardcore

1 Excavate the area to a depth of 10cm (4in) below the finished surface level.

2 Fill the area to a depth of approximately 7cm (3in) with hardcore and then compact it to 5cm (2in) using a manual roller or vibrating plate. This will provide a solid base for the gravel.

3 Fill the area with gravel until it reaches the surface level. Rake well to help settle the gravel. You may choose to roller the top layer to get a more compact surface.

Left This understated gravel path complements the colourful planting without detracting from it.

It is possible to lay a gravel area for pedestrian use without a hardcore base. This will enable you to create planting pockets into the earth below, as in the low-maintenance courtyard (see page 78). It is best to use a geo textile membrane under the gravel to keep weeds at bay. You could use the membrane under hardcore, too, but you will have less of a weed problem as the earth is not as accessible.

Excavate the area to a depth of 5cm (2in) below the finished surface level. Compact the ground (treading with your feet will be sufficient), cover the entire area with geotextile membrane and fill the area with gravel until it reaches the surface level.

With both methods you will find that the gravel settles, so you may need to top up the level at a later date.

Left Is this an informal path or a dry riverbed? Several sizes and colours are combined with striking success.

NATURAL STONE OR PRE-CAST SLABS

This is probably the most common type of paving and comes in a wide range of colours and sizes (see page 38–39). There are two methods of laying slabs: on a dry mix or a wet mix. The dry mix is suitable for any size of slab but particularly good for ones that are thin or small. Personally I find the dry mix much easier, but you will always find someone else who prefers wet. Some say it is easier to get the slabs level on wet mix. Either method takes a little practice.

Right Once it is laid, it's hard to tell manufactured york stone from real stone, especially when – as here – the planting settles the scheme into its surroundings.

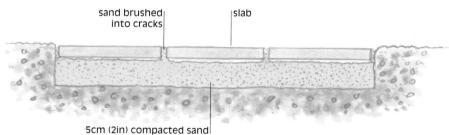

sand brushed into cracks | slab

5cm (2in) compacted sand

Dry laying

1 Excavate the area to a depth of 5cm (2in) plus the thickness of your slabs.

2 Fill the area with sand and compact with a vibrating plate to a depth of 5cm (2in).

3 Lay the slabs on the sand.

4 Brush kiln-dried sand into the cracks between the slabs.

Wet laying

1 As for dry laying.

2 Make up a mix of mortar using 1 measure of cement to 5 measures of soft sand and enough water to make the consistency of cream cheese.

3 Put five blobs of mortar on the ground where the slab is to go, one for each corner of the slab and one in the middle.

4 Place the slab on the mortar blobs.

5 Fill the cracks between with more of the mortar and brush the slabs clean before the mortar sets hard.

Stepping stones in a lawn

1 Choose slabs that are large enough to accommodate a large foot easily. Lay them out on top of the lawn and try them out: each slab should be a comfortable stride from the next.

2 Cut through the turf around each slab with a sharp knife.

3 Remove the slabs and, using a border space, lift the turf to a depth just deeper than your slab.

4 Spread a thin layer of sand in the bottom of each hole and place the slab on top. If necessary use extra sand to get the slab level.

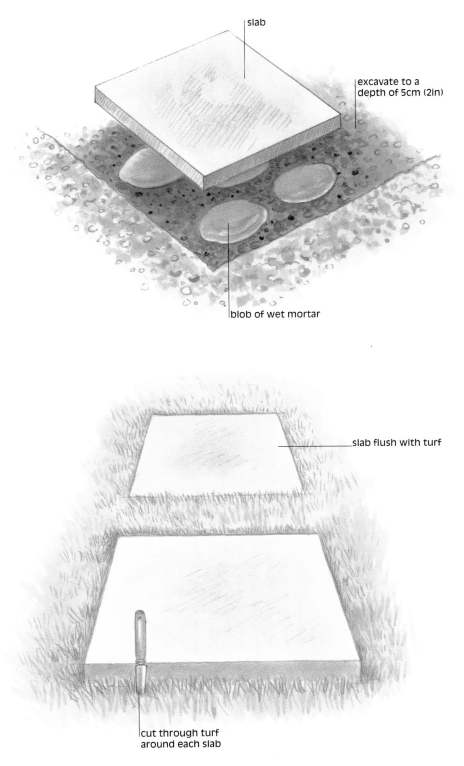

slab

excavate to a depth of 5cm (2in)

blob of wet mortar

slab flush with turf

cut through turf around each slab

TILES OR MOSAIC

This type of hard landscaping is becoming more and more popular as we lose our inhibitions about what is acceptable in the garden. Don't be afraid to experiment with colour and texture, but make sure that the materials you choose are suitable to withstand a winter outside; many tiles will be for interior use only and therefore not frostproof.

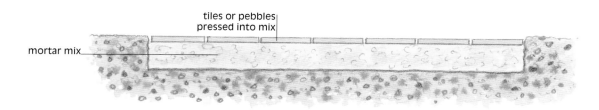

tiles or pebbles
pressed into mix

mortar mix

Right Using only two colours can be just as exciting as a multicoloured design. Use the shape of each pebble to accentuate the pattern, as the edging of this woven path does.

1 Excavate the area to a depth of 2cm (about 1in).

2 Make up a mortar mix of 1 measure of cement to 5 measures of sand and enough water to make the mixture the consistency of cream cheese.

3 Spread the mortar over the area to a depth of just under 2cm (¾in).

4 Press the tiles or pebbles into the mortar while the mix is still wet. You might find it helps to soak the tiles in clean water before you lay them. The skill level for laying this type of material is medium – more than anything it requires lots of patience, so take small areas at a time and don't rush.

CONCRETE

Once the poor relation of garden hard landscape, only used for areas of utility, concrete is now appreciated as a useful and stylish material. It is within most people's capabilities to mix concrete by hand if you only need a very small amount, but you would be wise to hire a mixer for larger quantities. However, if you are attempting a terrace or large path I would suggest you investigate purchasing a load of ready-mixed concrete; it will arrive in a lorry with a pouring arm to deliver its load exactly where you need it. Another advantage of using ready-mixed concrete is that the load will have a constant consistency. Unless you are very experienced, this is hard to achieve if you are mixing a series of smaller loads.

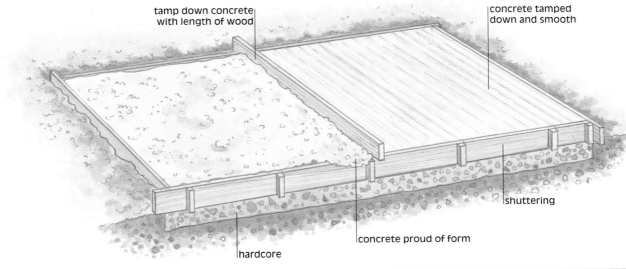

tamp down concrete with length of wood

concrete tamped down and smooth

shuttering

concrete proud of form

hardcore

1 Excavate the area to a depth of 15cm (6in).

2 Construct wooden shuttering around the area, if necessary, to act as a mould. (You will not need shuttering where the concrete runs up to a wall or other existing hard surface.)

3 Fill the area with a base of hardcore and compact it down to a depth of 7–8cm (3in).

4 Pour the concrete in and tamp it using a length of wood to ensure the mix settles evenly without air gaps and with a smooth surface.

A terrace wider than 3m (10ft) begins to get complicated, as you will have to leave spacing joints to allow for contraction. Also, a raft of concrete larger than this would not be suitable for an area of unstable ground or one prone to waterlogging.

Right This simple use of white concrete slabs and turf demonstrates that grass need never be mundane.

BRICKS, COBBLES OR BLOCK PAVING

Paving blocks come in many different varieties, and you can buy either natural stone cobbles or, less expensively, pre-cast cobbles. This type of laying requires a certain amount of skill but if you feel you are competent at practical projects then it is great fun. Once the groundwork is done the blocks go down so quickly you can see your hard work pay off. It is worth practising the pattern you are going to lay before you start to work on the real site. Consult your suppliers, too, as they will probably have a booklet offering a wide range of laying patterns.

The area will need to be surrounded by a firm edge restraint such as a building, kerb or purpose-made edging strip.

1 Excavate the area to a depth of 20cm (8in) from the finished ground level.

2 Fill the area with hardcore to a depth of 10cm (4in) and compact it using a vibrating plate.

3 Fill the area with sand to a depth of 5cm (2in) and compact using the vibrating plate.

4 Fill with more sand and level to leave a depth exactly the same as the paving you are to lay.

5 Lay your paving onto the sand in your chosen pattern. Brush kiln-dried sand over the whole area and pass a vibrating plate over to pack the sand tightly into the joints.

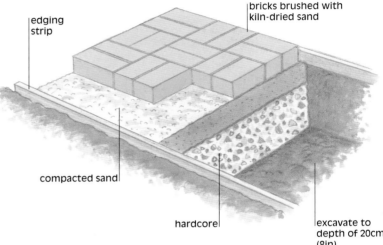

edging strip

bricks brushed with kiln-dried sand

compacted sand

hardcore

excavate to depth of 20cm (8in)

Right Old bricks look wonderful laid as paths, but make sure that they were originally used for paving and not for walls, as walling bricks are too soft and will break in frost.

BARK

This is a really useful and inexpensive material for the garden, used as paths and around play equipment, as a good safe and clean surface for children to run on. It can be laid with a structured edge, or just spread thickly in a woodland area, allowing the plants to come through as they want. These instructions are for an edged area with an underlayer of membrane to keep weeds at bay.

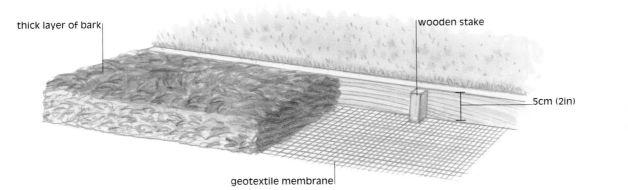

thick layer of bark   wooden stake

5cm (2in)

geotextile membrane

Below This border is softened by the bark path, allowing easy access without the hard edges of solid landscape.

1 Clear the area to a depth of 5cm (2in). Remove any large stones and tread the earth so that it is well compacted.

2 Make a groove around the edge of the area to a depth of 5cm (2in), then place timber lengths 10 x 2cm (4 x ¾in), on end in the groove. Hold in place with wooden stakes hammered into the earth on alternate sides of the board.

3 Cut some geotextile membrane to the size of the area and cover the earth, making sure that it goes right to the edge of the board.

4 Put a thick layer of bark chippings all over the surface. For a children's play area you will need to make the bark 10cm (4in) deep for safety.

The Practicalities of Hard Landscaping

INDEX

ACKNOWLEDGEMENTS

Editorial Manager: Jane Birch
Executive Art Editor: Peter Burt
Copy-editor: Caroline Ball
Designer: Mark Stevens
Illustrator: Gill Tomblin
Picture Researcher: Zoë Holtermann
Senior Production Controller: Ian Paton

PHOTOGRAPHIC ACKNOWLEDGEMENTS

Adrian Bloom Horticultural Library/Richard Bloom 44 bottom left.

Mark Bolton 34, 37 right, 41 bottom, 64 bottom, 116, 121 centre/Designer: Bradley Hole/The Telegraph Garden/RHS Chelsea Flower Show 2000 8, 23 left.

Jonathan Buckley/Stoneacre, Kent/Designer: Rosemary Alexander 19 top

Emap Gardening Picture Library 71 right, 71 centre, 99 bottom.

Garden Picture Library/Eric Crichton 14 left, /John Glover 31, 130, 133 bottom, /Jacqui Hurst 133 top, /Mayer/Le Scanff 7, 46 left, /John Miller 25 top, /Jerry Pavia 67 left, /Clay Perry 20 left, /Howard Rice 45 right, 67 right, 72 centre left, /Kevin Richardson 50, 64 centre, /JS Sira 45 left, 117, /Ron Sutherland/Designer: Anthony Paul 12.

John Glover 19 bottom, 20 right, 25 bottom, 26, 28, 42, 44 top left, 44 top right, 58 bottom, 64 top, 72 top right, 72 centre right, 83 right, /Designer: Nicholas Howard/RHS Hampton Court Flower Show 2001 104, /Designer: Peter Styles/RHS Chelsea Flower Show 1996 102, /Heathfield, Surrey 75, /Designer: Julie Toll/RHS Hampton Court Flower Show 1997 39 top left.

Octopus Publishing Group Limited/Mark Bolton/Designer: Christopher Costin/Scenic Design Landscaping/RHS Hampton Court Flower Show 2001 21 bottom, /Mark Bolton/Designer: Paul Dyer/Very Interesting Landscape & Water Feature Co./RHS Hampton Court Flower Show 2001 38 bottom right, /Mark Bolton/Designer: Simon Harmon/Lilies Water Gardens/RHS Hampton Court Flower Show 2001 39 bottom right, 139, /Mark Bolton/Designer: Tom Stuart-Smith/The Laurent-Perrier Harpers & Queen Garden/RHS Chelsea Flowers Show 2001 4,14 right, /Mark Winwood 18 bottom.

Robert Harding Picture Library/Steve Bavister 125, /Garden Inspirations 1, 23 right, 48 left.

Jerry Harpur 47 left, /Cordoba Patio Festival (Conoce los Patios Cordobeses), Spain 136, /Designer: Topher Delaney 24, /Designer: Simon Fraser, Middx 16 Bottom/Simon Fraser, Middx 38 bottom left, /Designer: Sonny Garcia, San Francisco, CA 36 right, /Kyoto Temple, Japan 38 top left, /Shore Hall, Essex 21 top, /Designer: Tim Du Val, NYC 17 Top, /RHS Wisley 96, /York Gate, Leeds 15 bottom.

Marcus Harpur 71 left, /Cressing Temple, Essex, 78-79, 86/RHS Hampton Court Flower Show 2000 36 left, /Designer: Tom Stuart-Smith for Chanel/RHS Chelsea Flower Show 1998 10, /Designer: Stephen Woodhams 48 right.

Hugh Palmer 46 right, /House & Garden /Cartier Garden /RHS Chelsea Flower Show 1994 13 right.

Andrew Lawson 30, 109, /Designer: Arabella Lennox-Boyd 58 Top, /Designer: Anthony Noel 82-83 centre, /Designer: Ryl Nowell/Wilderness Farm 134, /Designer: Phillippa O'Brien/RHS Hampton Court Flower Show 2000 39 bottom left, /Designer: Mirabel Osler 16 top, /Designer: Jane Sweetser/Still Water & Dreams, RHS Hampton Court Flower Show 1999 17 bottom, /Designer: Kathy Swift, Morville, Shropshire 129, /York Gate, Leeds 128.

Clive Nichols 89, /Boardman Gelly & Co. 11 bottom, /Garden and Security Lighting 77, /Hadspen Garden, Somerset 18 top, /Designers: Trevyn McDowell & Paul Thompson 93, /Designer: Jane Sweetser 91.

Jerry Pavia 44 bottom right.

Purves & Purves/www.purves.co.uk/tel: 0207 580 8223 105.

Derek St Romaine 22.

J S Sira 120.

Jo Whitworth/RHS Chelsea Flower Show 2000 11 top.

Rob Whitworth/RHS Gardens, Wisley 113, /Designers: Jeremy Salt and Roger Bullock/RHS Hampton Court Flower Show 2000 106, 121 top.

Steven Wooster 99 top,/Designer: Allison Armour/Homes & Gardens Magazine/RHS Chelsea Flower Show 2000 13 left,/A garden in Auckland, NZ, designer: Rod Barnett 2,/Pippa Bishops's Garden, Auckland, NZ 138,/Cottonwood, NZ 15 top/Craigholm, Hunterville, NZ 37 left,/The Dillon Garden, Dublin, R.O.I 47 right,/Designer: Nan Raymond/Ethridge Gardens, Timaru, NZ 40,/Jack Richard's Garden, Wainui Beach, NZ 41 top,/Designer: Annie Wilkes, Sydney, Australia 39 top right, 137.